SUPERSTAR

SUPERSTAR

A Hip Chick's Guide to the Top

Rachel Bell

Illustrated by Nicola Slater

2 PALMER STREET, FROME, SOMERSET BA11 1DF

Thank you to Vic and Dean, Lauren, Pete, Chris, Mikey, Rach and David, Mum,
Carl, Mr. Marsh and everyone I interviewed.

First published in Great Britain in 2000
The Chicken House
2 Palmer Street
Frome, Somerset BA11 1DF
United Kingdom

Cover design by Tony Potter Publishing Ltd
Designed and typeset by Dorchester Typesetting Group Ltd
Printed and bound in Great Britain.

British Library Cataloguing in Publication data available.
Library of Congress Cataloging in Publication Data available.

ISBN 1-903434-04-1

Contents

Introduction

Have you always wanted to be on TV? Think you could show the Spice Girls a thing or two? Maybe you're wild about animals or maybe you're an ace on the tennis court! Whatever your passion, whatever your talent, there's a job out there for you! Welcome to your essential guide to cool careers, jammy jobs and making your dreams come true!

From training and getting started to do's and don'ts and nabbing that big break, I'm here to tell you everything you never knew about exciting jobs! And don't worry if you're not sure what you want to do – I'll be revealing

the inside story on a whole heap of careers, getting the low-down on real life in the fast lane and bagging all the best tips from the top!

Careers aren't just about skills and qualifications – your personality plays a big part, too! That's why I've compiled a Personality Quiz to help you discover your hidden talents, make the most of your strengths and reveal the kind of job that suits you. It won't tell you what to do with your life, but it will give you lots of inspiration and get you thinking about what it is that makes you tick.

Don't settle for being just a dreamer. If you try something you'll find out if you really like it or not, whereas if you never try, you'll never really know and you may always wonder, "What if . . .?" Remember, as with almost everything else in life, when it comes to talent and careers, practice makes perfect. Just go ahead and start now. No matter how small the step, start from where you are. The more you do, the more experience you'll have to help you decide what you really want to do in the long run.

And once you find what you really want to do, you'll gain the confidence that comes from experience. Then, stand back world; there'll be no stopping you! One day I may be asking you for your autograph, or bringing my dog to you so you can make her well, or maybe you'll save my house from burning down . . . You get the picture.

Just remember, everyone who has made a success of her career is just a person, like you. And once, they were girls with big ambitions, just like you. So whether you want to travel the world, save lives or see your name in lights, go get 'em girl!

A recent survey by The Guide Association, asked girls from all backgrounds about their hopes and dreams. It found that 99 percent of 11-17 year olds believe it is up to them to make their lives successful and 75 percent believe they are in control of their future. "Today's girl is more ambitious, more confident and more adventurous than ever before. One thing is clear about girls growing up in the 21st century — they want it all!"

The Guide Association, May 2000

She's Gotta Have It!

"I want to be a professional blader. My brothers are all bladers and they think I'm really good. Sadly, I'll have to go and live in the States as there aren't the same opportunities for bladers in Britain yet. There's nothing else I want to do."

EMMA GREENWOOD, 12

"I'd like to be the manager of a major retail store because I like clothes, money and being in charge. I think I'll do a degree in Law or Accountancy as that's the way to get to the top."

JENNY STEVENSON, 15

"I want to be a solo singer like Britney Spears! I'm a good dancer. My more realistic choice would be to work in a dog kennels and be a dog handler because I'm mad about pets."

MARIA ROBERTS, 14

"I've lived around farms all my life and I really love animals. I want to work for the RSPCA and rescue small animals like dogs and cats. I hate to see animals get hurt."

CHARLOTTE ROBERTS, 12

"I want to be an actress. It's not for the money; its because I love acting. I'd like to be in TV and films but the money would be a bonus."

LUCY MAYLOR, 14

"I want to be an actress because I want to be on TV. I wouldn't mind being a presenter, but I'd rather be in a soap."

MICHAELA DONNELLY, 11

"I want to be an art teacher. My mum's an art teacher and I'm really good at art. But what I really want to be is an animator."

JESSICA SEATON, 14

"I really want to be a vet but I'll probably end up as a music teacher. I do music as a hobby and everybody says I'm really good at it. My parents keep saying, 'Why don't you become a music teacher?' – but I really like being outside, I love animals and I really want to be a vet."

ANNA EARLE, 16

SHE'S GOTTA HAVE IT!

"In the US, football is totally accepted as a sport for both men and women. My dream is to play for a well-known football team in the US, play with the best players in the world and be known as a great football player. I'd prefer it if England was as professional, then I could play for my country and play in front of my friends and see my family. I'd like to come over here sometimes, like Kelly Smith, who plays for the England National Squad, and then, coach."

BETH SIMM, 16

"I'm good at Mathematics and Science and I think I'll go to college or university to study Biology. I haven't really decided what I want to do after that. It will probably be to do with the environment."

BECKY LITTLETON, 16

"I'm really into fashion – not all that designer stuff; I'm talking about second-hand stuff, collector's items, you know. I'd like to have my own boutique, the sort of place people come when they want something totally original."

GLORIA STERNHAM, 16

"I think I'd like to be a lawyer. I like the idea of helping people and doing something important. I think women are good at understanding people's needs and not judging them immediately."

DEBBIE ROYLE, 15

"When I leave school I want to travel; you know, get one of those round-the-world tickets. I know loads of people who just work in bars or camps or hostels for a few months and then move on. I'm a bit scared about going on my own but I'd meet loads of people."

SALLY BECKLEY, 14

"I'd like to have a vegetarian café with my mate, Rachel. We've worked in a lot of restaurants together so I reckon we'd make a pretty good team. I'd have to do all the cooking though. She could do the drinks!"

KAREN TONGE, 13

SHE'S GOTTA HAVE IT!

"I'm not sure what I want to be. Being the singer in a really cool girl band?! I'd want to play guitar too, but I can't be bothered to learn! I'm a bit lazy like that."

SALLY STUART, 15

"Well last year I wanted to be an architect and now I'm thinking about being a graphic designer. I'd like to design graphics for TV."

KATE SANDERS, 16

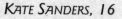

"All I know is I want to study Languages at university. I'll decide later if I'm going to live and work abroad."

BETHANY GRANT, 14

"I'd like to be a pilot. I think the whole thing is still a bit sexist because when I tell people, they don't take me seriously. But I'm serious all right."

KIRSTY MOORE, 15

"Thinking up ideas for commercials sounds like fun. You could be really silly. I'm quite creative so I think I'd be good at it."

TARA WOODS, 13

"I don't know what I want to do. When I was really little I wanted to be a nurse. Most girls think that, don't they? All I know is I want to do something worthwhile; maybe working with animals, maybe working for a charity."

SAM CRAIG, 12

"I love making my own jewelry. I know you can do courses in jewelry design but I know my dad wouldn't be into it. He still doesn't think art is a proper subject!"

KELLY TUTURRO, 15

SHE'S GOTTA HAVE IT!

Wh☺ Am I?

Choosing a career is a big decision and not something to hurry. Don't worry if you haven't got a clue what you want to do yet. These stars probably never imagined they'd be where they are today!

1 The actress who made three of the scariest movies ever, Scream 1,2 and 3, had her heart set on a totally different career in her school days – but who is she?

"I was never going to be an actor. I was going to be a classical ballerina. This all just happened."

There's plenty of time to make up your mind! This hugely successful TV presenter and radio DJ was forever changing her tune! She wanted to be:

"1. A ballerina. 2. An all-singing, dancing brat. 3. A Bond girl."

 3 Some of the world's biggest success stories absolutely hated school, including this talented diva with an attitude. These days she's like a blast of fresh air in the safe and predictable pop charts:

"Before I went to fame school in New York, I went to a private school, which I hated. I just felt like it wasn't for me. The problem I have with the school system is that they make all kids learn in the same way. I wasn't stupid. But there was nothing to inspire me to learn."

4

I bet this girl never dreamed she'd be in the biggest girl group in the world and a role model to millions!

"At 16, I'd just started college to study Travel and Tourism. I was more consumed by my immediate future. It was more, 'Am I going to get a big spot on my nose the day before that big party!'"

This WNBA superstar had it all worked out when she was a kid. And sports weren't even on the agenda!

5

"No, I didn't always want to be a basketball player. When I was younger I wanted to be a weather reporter and a model."

6

This animal mad actress wanted to be a zoologist when she was a kid and never imagined she'd be making Hollywood movies with the likes of Ewan McGregor, Jim Carey and Al Pacino. Can you guess who's talking?

"I've always loved animals. When I was growing up I had two snakes. The bigger one was about six feet long and I raised mice for them to eat. I also had three dogs, three cats and five birds. I always thought I'd get a job working with animals."

WHO AM I?

7

She starred in one of the most successful movies ever made, with the world's favorite poster boy. So who is this down-to-earth girl?

"I never ever really set out to become famous, rich, well known and respected, or anything like that."

8

This girl knew what she wanted on her first day at school. And it didn't involve presenting the UK's favorite Saturday morning show!

"When I was six I wanted to be Julie Andrews. Then I ended up at this really academic grammar school where everyone wanted to be lawyers or doctors. So I did my exams and realized I still wanted to be Julie Andrews!"

Answers: 1 Neve Campbell, 2 Zoe Ball, 3 Kelis, 4 Geri Halliwell, 5 Lisa Leslie. 6 Cameron Diaz, 7 Kate Winslet 8 Cat Deeley

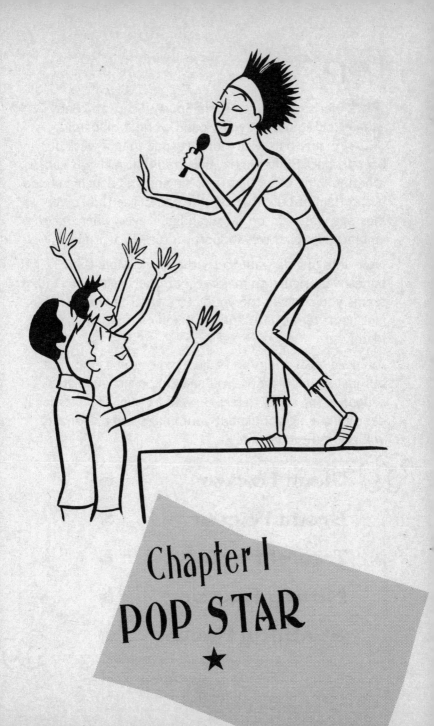

Chapter 1
POP STAR
★

Pop Star

Ever since Ginger, Posh, Sporty, Scary and Baby rocked our cozy boy band world, bombarding planet pop with more attitude than a week of back-to-back Buffy, we have realized that real girls can do it better. Who cares that their singing and dancing are no better than our own? That's the point. The Girl Power message was right on target and girls everywhere have embraced its positive, supportive, can-do attitude.

Now, lots of girls want to try their luck. More than 32 girl bands were signed to major record labels last year. And, it seems you're never too young to start. The world is on first name terms with Britney, Brandy, Christina and Mandy.

You need great songs and a good voice to be a pop star, but just as importantly, you need to be a charismatic performer. The ability to keep up with a troupe of professional dancers is a big bonus, but your image and personality will get you everywhere.

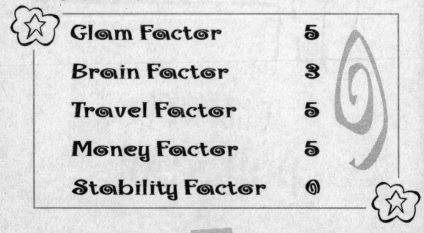

Glam Factor	5
Brain Factor	3
Travel Factor	5
Money Factor	5
Stability Factor	0

Have I Got the Right Personality for the Job?

Just look at the Spice Girls! They are so successful because they are five big personalities and every one of them is different.

"To make a good pop group, you need lots of different personalities that appeal to lots of different people, like a daring one, a charming one and a quiet and interesting one. You've got to have a good mix so they appeal to everybody."

PETE MOUNTSTEVENS, MUSIC PR

Image and personality are all-important. To get noticed and become successful, you have got to be a celebrity as well as an artist. Having a different look and your own image will make you stand out. Geri Haliwell's bright red hair got her noticed and it's as much a part of her success as her big personality is!

This is a job that takes 100 percent commitment and dedication. All those long hours traveling between interviews and photo shoots will tire you out, but you must always be enthusiastic and friendly. If people don't like you, you won't go far. They won't put you in their magazine, they won't ask you to come on their show and they won't play your records!

And if you want to be a solo artist, you have to be able to carry the whole show by yourself! You must be super-confident and outgoing because you'll be meeting lots of new people on a regular basis. From interviews with music journalists to chatting on the couch with MTV presenters, it's your job to sell yourself. You've got to have something to say and attitude is where it's at!

"You've got to want to be famous. Never mind maybe. It's 'Yes, I am going to make it.' Image is important, but you've got to have a vision and a drive to succeed."

JOANNA BURNS, SENIOR
EXECUTIVE, EPIC PRESS

Getting Started

You don't need any formal qualifications, but getting a good education is still important. We've all heard the phrase One Hit Wonder. You'll need some way to support yourself until you're discovered. The more clued-up you are about the music industry, the better, so talk to anyone and everyone you can find who's working in the industry.

There are schools that specialize in courses on music, singing, dancing and acting, as well as music technology, recording, and composing. But don't think that this will get you out of studying English and Science. Students in these schools study all the academic stuff, too. So, in many ways, these schools are more demanding.

Competition to get in is fierce and you need to be able to prove that you have talent in your chosen area of study.

A couple of the famous stage schools are The Sylvia Young Theatre School in London, where Baby Spice prepared for world domination and La Guardia in New York, where Kelis learned to write and belt out a tune! Some students come from miles around and stay with local families, others just attend classes on Saturdays.

But you don't have to go to stage school. If you can sing, dance, play an instrument or write songs, you're in with a chance. Join a singing or dance class after school or at weekends. Get as much experience as possible by performing at school, at friends' parties or doing karaoke! Everybody starts small so get as many gigs as you can in your area.

The trick is to create a buzz by getting as many people as possible to hear you. Record yourself on tape, send it to the local radio station and get some feedback. Hundreds of acts send their tapes to record companies and managers. If you can find a manager first, the record companies are much more likely to give your tape a listen. The Music Week or Billboard directory, published once a year, lists the names of managers and record companies. Check out music/entertainment papers like NME, Melody Maker and The Stage. They

POP STAR

advertise bands looking for singers and auditions for new groups. That's how the Spice Girls got together!

If you're sending a tape to a record company, send it to the A&R (Artists and Repertoire) department. You'll find addresses in the sleeves of your CDs, too. The A&R departments look for and sign new acts. If you've got a gig, invite the A&R scout along. But, they see a lot of these letters, so don't be surprised if they don't turn up.

My Big Break

Lene Marlin writes and performs her own songs and plays guitar. Here's how it all happened for Norway's most talented teen! "My first big break came in a very strange way. A friend of mine had heard me play and got me into the local radio station in Tromso, where I live. Someone heard me play a few songs and called Virgin Records in Oslo. They called me and asked for a tape of my music. The next thing I knew, I was being flown to Oslo and signed to a record deal. It was when I was in Virgin, surrounded by loads of demo tapes other people had sent in, that I realized how lucky I was."

Singer/songwriter Jewel grew up on a farm in Alaska and moved to California when she was 18. She played guitar in small clubs and had very little money before her big break came along.

Jessica Simpson started singing in church. When the Sony chairman who signed up Mariah Carey heard Jessica, she got a record contract! "My father's a minister so I grew up singing gospel and I just fell in love with it. I would perform after he preached, sometimes in front of 30,000 people."

Mandy Moore says she started her career, "jumping up and down on my bed singing." It was at a summer music camp, that Mandy, aged nine, decided she wanted to sing. "My parents thought it was just a phase I'd grow out of, but I stuck to it and begged them for acting and voice lessons."

At 8, Christina Aguilera performed on a TV show called *Star Search*. At 12, she landed a spot on the biggest kid's TV show in America, *The Mickey Mouse Club*. She was a lead performer with a backing band on the show, made up of Justin N'Sync and some girl called Britney!

Do's and Don'ts

Do: Get a good education because you'll need a good job to pay your rent and buy your food until you get your big break. Remember, making it as a pop star takes luck and even the most talented artists don't always make it. So, prepare yourself to make a decent living while you work toward your main goal.

Do: If you're sending a tape to an A&R department, include a photo. Your image counts as much as your talent. Also include copies of articles about yourself from your home town newspaper, any posters and programs from gigs and shows you may have done, and a short bio that focuses on your performance experiences and aspirations.

Do: Visit getoutthere.bt.com where you're given the tools to upload music onto the Web. Let A&R departments know if they can download your music off the Web (although few bands have been signed this way).

Do: Get as much experience in as possible by joining local music/singing groups and performing whenever you can.

Don't: Be taken in by dishonest managers promising to make you famous. Stick to those listed in the Music Week or Billboard directories.

Don't: Compromise your ambitions, talent or morals for anyone.

> *"We were doing a photo shoot and the stylist wanted me to wear a pair of tiny hot pants that my bottom was hanging out of. She was, like, 'They make you look skinny and everyone's wearing them,' and I said, 'Good for them, but I'm not looking like that.'"*
>
> ANIKA BOSTELAAR, 18, GIRL THING

Don't: Send a tape of you singing a Mariah Carey or Whitney Houston song. No one can perform their songs better than they can, so make sure your material is original or not well-known.

Don't: Expect success overnight. There are hundreds of hopefuls out there and it may take a long time and a LOT of hard work before you are noticed.

The Girl Thing Story

Girl Thing was signed up by RCA records executive, Simon Cowell and Chris Herbert, who used to be the Spice Girls' manager!

All five girls are from stage school or performing backgrounds and were brought together via auditions or recommendations from the likes of Sylvia Young.

Pink haired Michelle, 21, was working in a café in Blackpool and doing shows in the summer season. Linzi, 19, was singing with her dad's karaoke act around Manchester, and Jodi, now 16, quit stage school at 15 to join the group. Nikki, 20, and Anika, 18, also went to stage school.

The girls were given a house to share so they could do some girl bonding. "We argued a lot at first, but we are very close now. And although we are all very different, we share the same ambitions," says Jodi. And they don't care if people criticize them for being manufactured. "If anything, we're proud to be the chosen ones," says Nikki.

"We're using the same songwriters who worked with the Spice Girls," admits Michelle. "Yes, we have followed exactly the same path as them, but if it's not broken, why fix it? It's almost impossible to be a completely original act, but that doesn't mean you can't be a good act."

Hours

This is no 9-5 job! You could be working 12 hours a day for months without a day off. You could be traveling between five different countries and doing ten photo shoots or TV appearances all in one week. When you're starting out, you'll have to work extra hard to get as much exposure as possible. And once you're famous, you will have to work even harder to stay on top!

For all the glamour, this is no easy job and you'll be away from family and friends for long periods, especially if you're touring. Britney and Christina Aguilera have both been advised by their doctors to cancel tours because of overwork.

> "You're always traveling and away from home. Last year S Club 7 worked New Year's Eve and New Year's Day. I think Christmas Day was their only day off!"
>
> PETER LORRAINE, ARTIST DEVELOPMENT MANAGER, POLYDOR RECORDS

Salary

You need consistent success to make really big money. A hit single is not enough. You need consistently successful, chart-topping albums. The money a record makes is called "royalties" and it's split between the band's members. If you write the songs, or get involved in the song writing, like Shaznay All Saint, you'll earn even more.

A pop act never makes any money until they have paid their record company back all it has invested in them. The record company pays for your videos, stylists, clothes, travel; everything. So first of all, the money from your hits will be used to pay the record company back. Then, if you are successful enough, you can start the serious shopping! However, if you never even sell a single and your act flops, you don't have to pay the record company back. It's up to them to take those investment risks.

Perks and Pitfalls

Perk: The buzz of fulfilling your dream. People will pay to come and see you perform and you'll hear your songs on the radio!

Perk: If you're successful, you can earn massive amounts of money.

Perk: The parties! You can gawp at celebs and meet all the interesting creative people working behind the scenes.

Perk: You get to travel all over the world.

Perk: The freebies are way cool, from clothes to holidays.

Perk: Having your own stylist and make-up artist. With money ANYONE can look a million dollars, baby!

Pitfall: The hours stink! The more famous you become, the more hours you have to work (and that includes lots of early mornings, too).

Pitfall: Long periods away from home, friends and family.

> "When I started recording it was hard. My friends didn't understand why I couldn't hang out with them."
>
> MANDY MOORE, 16

Pitfall: You're always in the public eye and you lose a lot of privacy. To sustain your public image, you've got to be polite and cheery all the time (what a drag!).

Pitfall: Newspapers make up stories and gossip about you and they watch everything you do.

Short Cuts to the Top

This is one business where you can jump right up to the top. But only if:

* You know someone famous.

* Someone famous writes you a song.

* You're a model, TV presenter or actress first. Record companies will give you a deal much faster if you're on TV already!

◎ Tip from the Top ◎

> "You need talent but you also need opportunities. You've got to be in the right place at the right time. To really make it, you've got to have stamina, energy and determination."
>
> SYLVIA YOUNG, FOUNDER OF THE SYLVIA YOUNG THEATRE SCHOOL

Other Careers in the Music Business

In the 90s, DJs became the new superstars and loads of kids are switching their guitars for decks. But the music industry has loads of cool jobs to offer and many talented people, including a few wannabe pop stars and musicians, work behind the scenes.

Another good starting point is getting work experience at a record company, with a view to becoming a full-time Press Officer. Press Officers write artists' biographies and press releases, and set up interviews with magazines. It's necessary to have a wide knowledge of music and good writing skills. Look in Music Week for jobs on offer and check out the Music Week directory for names of record companies and independent PR companies to contact. Record companies take graduate trainees but you can get a job by writing an original application telling them why they should employ you, proving your musical knowledge and asking for an informal chat.

Joanna Burns, now senior executive of Epic Press, has helped launch the careers of Mandy Moore, B*Witched, Charlotte Church and Celine Dion to name a few.

POP STAR

"I started here as a secretary and worked my way up. I was a regional press officer, then head of press and now I'm senior. There are great opportunities for secretaries to get promoted."

A TV Plugger gets artists on TV, a Radio Plugger gets them airplay, and the Artists & Repertoire department looks for and signs new talent. They also nurture and launch artists.

There are loads of creative jobs, including Video Commissioner, who dreams up the idea for a video, and Video Director. A record company's art department comes up with ideas for album covers and the marketing department sells the artist to the public.

Does all this sound like something you WANT to do, but you feel like it's all a bit too much to seriously consider? Don't worry, a lot of other girls feel just the same! But, remember: the more you do, the more you'll learn. With enough experience you'll be able to decide if it's what you really want, and then, with enough hard work AND a lot of luck you'll have as much of a chance for success as anyone.

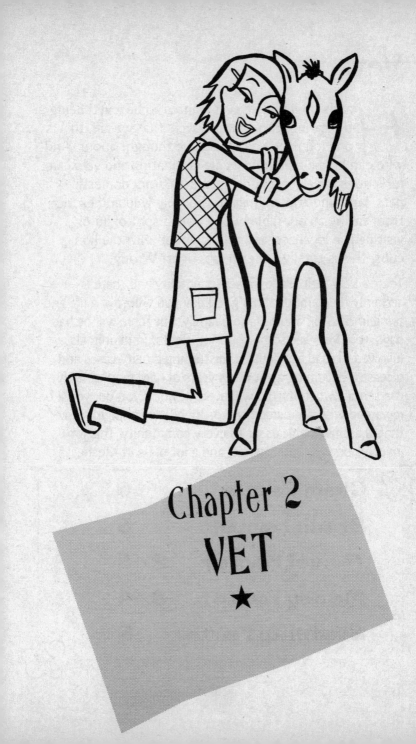

Chapter 2
VET
★

Vet

Hands up if you've ever wanted to be a vet! Being the caring, cool animal lovers that we are, this is one job nearly all of us have thought about. And who can blame us? Animals are fascinating and vets care for a huge variety of cuddly creatures, from domestic pets, farm and zoo animals to the truly wild and exotic. From saving an adorable puppy from a spot of flu or visiting the local zoo and rolling about with the lion cubs, this is totally a dream job, right? Wrong.

There's very little place for sentimentality and there is certainly no glamour. On a good day you will save a life and bring immense happiness to a family, but there will be bad days, too. Vets see some shocking sights, from animals involved in road accidents to disturbing cruelty cases and diseases. Becoming a vet takes years of hard work so only the seriously committed will make it. But if you do, you'll be rewarded with an incredibly worthwhile, meaningful career that is an invaluable asset to every community. This job involves bravery, intelligence, and a lot of heart. Respect.

Glam Factor	0
Brain Factor	5
Travel Factor	2/3
Money Factor	3/4
Stability Factor	5

Have I Got the Right Personality for the Job?

Obviously, a love of animals is the reason most girls dream about becoming a vet. You have to be a strong character who cares about the welfare of animals. But you can't be too sentimental and you can't be squeamish about them at all. Vets see a lot of sick animals in terrible conditions. So if someone brings in a mangled puppy that's been run over by a car, bursting into tears or screaming at the sight of blood is not an option. You've got to be practical, observant, responsible and calm in a crisis. You've also got to give all animals (not just the cute, furry ones!) equal care.

Being a vet is as much about meeting people as it is about animals. So, not only do you need to love animals, you've got to like people, too!

> *"I wanted to become a vet because I loved animals more than people. But you meet new people all day. Nobody tells you about that side of the job. You certainly don't learn how to deal with people at vet school."*
>
> JULIA HARPER, VET

Patience, being self-assertive and good at communicating are also important qualities. You'll have to deal with owners getting upset, or even crying; the occasional pet owner will even throw a hissy fit. No matter what, though, you'll need to show concern, gain their trust and explain what's happening to their animal. And if you start your own private practice, you'll need a head for business, too.

You also need to be able to work hard and be determined to reach your goal. It takes A LOT of hard work to get into vet school so you need to be focused from an early age. If you're afraid of hard work, forget it.

Getting Started

Sorry sister, but grades are everything! Loads of young people want to be vets but veterinary science is one of the hardest college courses to get on. You need to stay on at school and get really good grades in three science subjects, such as chemistry, physics, biology and zoology. Mathematics is also a preferred subject. Then you'll need to do a veterinary science degree, which takes at least five years and often more. Even if you've got excellent grades, there is no guarantee you'll get in because competition for places is high. This really is a job for the determined, so pay attention to your education from an early age.

The high academic standard required is hardly surprising when you think of the huge range of animals a vet must know about. One patient might be a domestic pet, the next a farm animal, and even zoo animals and other very exotic creatures may come your way. Vets have to be surgeons, anaesthetists, pharmacists and GPs all at once.

Most colleges like you to have done a lot of work experience before you apply for their course. Some require it. So start filling your weekends and holidays now! Offer to help out at your local vet's, on a local farm, at your nearest zoo, or animal shelter or do volunteer work at an animal charity. From cleaning kennels and walking dogs to mucking out the pigs' stys, it all counts. However, assisting a vet is the most important experience you can get and it will help you decide if veterinary work really is the career for you.

"We get a lot of girls coming in to do work experience. They say they really love animals but they mean fluffy bunnies and kittens with bows. They refuse to mop up the vomit, clean out cages and faint at the sight of blood. A lot of them do one day and never come back!"

KIM FERGUS, SENIOR VETERINARY NURSE

Do's and Don't's

Do: Get lots of practical experience handling animals and ask for a placement at your local vet's. The more experience you've got, the better your chances of getting into vet school/university. Start today!

Do: Get used to handling people, too. Vets deal with new people every day and often they're upset and they're not always nice.

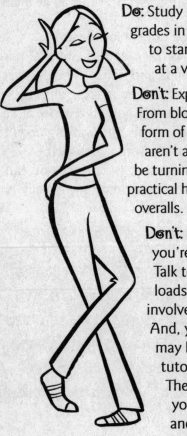

Do: Study hard. You'll need excellent grades in science in higher level exams to stand a chance of being accepted at a veterinary school/university.

Don't: Expect glamour from this career. From blood, puke, and every other form of waste and body fluid, animals aren't always delightful! And you'll be turning up for work with a very practical hairstyle, short fingernails and overalls. Mmm, stylish!

Don't: Lose heart if you don't think you're good enough at science. Talk to a career advisor. There are loads of jobs out there that involve working with animals! And, your advisor or counsellor may be able to help you get some tutoring to bring up your grades. The most important thing is your own determination, focus and hard work.

Why a Vet's Job can be a Fairytale

"One day someone brought in a dog that had been knocked over and mangled in a car's wheels. The poor thing was in a terrible state and we all expected it to die. But he surprised us and recovered. He'd lost a leg but he was such a little charmer. He was the happiest three legged dog alive!"

KIM FERGUS, SENIOR VETERINARY NURSE

Why a Vet's Job can be a Nightmare

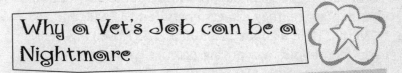

"You have to be prepared for people getting angry or upset if their animal isn't improving or can't be saved. I had to put one woman's cat to sleep. It was pretty old and had heart failure. She totally blamed me and sent me hate mail for two years! We laugh at it now, but it wasn't funny at the time. It was very upsetting."

JULIA HARPER, VET

Hours

They're long. You're on-call 24 hours a day. You'll have lots of early mornings and finish late in the evening, too. You must be prepared to get up at 4 a.m. for a sick animal. Every veterinary surgeon has an obligation to deal with emergencies in any species at any time. Get the picture?

However, if you work in a group practice, there will be a rota system so each vet is only on-call a few times a week and responsibilities are shared. Most vets see their role as a way of life, not a 9-5 job.

Salary

Vets have a good standard of living. It does vary but, in a group practice, they can earn between £17,000 and £25,000 (that's about $25,500 and $37,500) a year. If you've got your own private practice, you can earn up to £100,000 (about $150,000) a year. And if you become a TV vet, you'll be rolling in it!

Perks and Pitfalls

Perk: Treating an animal successfully is hugely rewarding.

Perk: You could be treating all kinds of animals, from exotic birds, lion cubs and chimps to horses, dolphins and dogs!

Perk: Variety. No two days are the same and you'll meet all kinds of animals and people.

> *"I enjoy meeting the people as much as the animals. From farmers who only have an economic interest, to the really keen pet breeders and families, you meet everyone!"*

STEPHEN BARABASH, VET

Pitfall: Treating sick animals can be upsetting but you can never show it.

Pitfall: The work is often dirty, smelly and physically demanding.

Pitfall: The long hours. Being on-call reduces your freedom to do other things.

◎ Tip from the Top ◎

"You have to like people as well as animals. To be sure you're making the right decision, go and work with as many vets as you can and get as much practical experience as possible. Without practical experience, you might only see the rosy side of it so be aware of the behind-the-scenes stuff, the stuff that is not so glamorous."

STEPHEN BARABASH, VET

VET

Short Cut to the Top

There aren't any short cuts to a veterinary qualification, but you make sure you're prepared with a good education in the right subjects and you can get as much practical experience through volunteer work as possible. That way, you'll be best placed to get the most out of your college work.

Other Careers in Veterinary Practice and Animal Welfare

There are loads of other ways to work with animals. Veterinary nurses work in private veterinary practices, animal hospitals and charities. They work with vets in the same way as nurses work with doctors. They do everything from cleaning and feeding to performing minor surgery, such as stitches, dental cleaning, taking X-rays and blood samples plus a bit of paperwork. You need to pass at least five subjects with good grades, including math or science. Or you can start with the pre-veterinary nursing certificate. This isn't a well-paid job and you can't work your way up to become a vet, without doing a proper veterinary science degree.

Animal charities need loads of animal lovers from inspectors, drivers, field workers, kennel workers, dog handlers, as well as fund-raisers and press officers, who raise awareness of the charity in magazines and newspapers.

Working in zoos or safari parks is an area with jobs at all levels, from zoologists to zookeepers and administrative staff. If you've thought about being a teacher, you could be an education officer, who makes sure schools know all about their local zoo and show children around.

Ask your careers advisor for more info on working with animals. Meanwhile, you might want to consider becoming any of these: Veterinary receptionist, dog trainer for seeing eye dogs and police dogs, pet shop worker, game keeper, riding instructor, groom, stable girl, cattery worker, or animal rights campaigner. Remember, there are always loads of opportunities to do volunteer work, at any age!

A wish to help, a love of animals, an ability to empathize and be patient with people whose animals are ill or hurt; these are all qualities important to successful veterinary practice. Hard work, dedication, and responsibility are also required, as is a certain kind of bravery that means you are the strong one when the chips are down. If these are personal qualities that describe you, then you deserve everyone's respect and thanks, and that's exactly what you're likely to get! So, don't let all the warnings about 'realism' put you off. If you have these skills to offer, and that's where your heart is, then go for it, girl!

Go for it!

VET

Chapter 3
MAGAZINE
EDITOR
★

Magazine Editor

I f the thought of starting your own magazine, running stories on everything and everyone that inspires you and seeing it all come together in a cool, glossy package on newstands across the globe makes you giddy with excitement, then you've probably thought about being an editor. And if you're creative, original and bursting with ideas, you're half way there! From interviewing stars and schmoozing at launch parties to invitations every night of the week, you'd be right to think of this job as a ticket to the glam life. But that's just a tiny part of it. A magazine editor must be clued up to fast moving social trends and popular culture, able to think on her feet, make important decisions and take all the flack. And did I mention all that hard work?

Glam Factor	3
Brain Factor	4
Travel Factor	3
Money Factor	4
Stability Factor	2-4

Have I Got the Right Personality for the Job?

The good news is that your ideas and your personality, not the number of exams you've passed, count for more in this profession. Being a magazine editor requires enthusiasm, dedication, and commitment. You must be prepared to work under pressure for long hours in order to meet all those deadlines. But to get noticed, you'll need lots of original ideas and be able to convince other people how good they are. Sell yourself, baby!

You'll also need to be well organized, motivated, good at communicating with others and taking responsibility. This is a management role, not a writing one, and you'll have a whole team of writers and designers looking to you for guidance!

"You can't make off-hand comments or be sarcastic because everybody takes you at your word. You're not one of the team. It's a big responsibility."

LAURA LEE DAVIES, 34, EDITOR OF TIME OUT, LONDON

"It's really difficult to find the balance between overseeing the creative side and keeping the vision of the magazine and making sure a staff of 18, all of whom have individual needs, are happy."

LAURI BERGER, EDITOR IN CHIEF OF JUMP, US

Editing is all about making contacts, too, so being confident and assertive really helps. With a bit of charm thrown in, you're laughing. Get out there and network!

Getting Started

There's no guaranteed route to becoming a magazine editor – some editors have long lists of qualifications on paper, others have none. A good education, especially passing your English exams and having a good understanding of English grammar will certainly help you. Editors read everything in the magazine and oversee the proof-readers who correct it.

Editors rewrite articles, too, so it's important to have good writing skills. Ask your English teacher to help you build these strengths.

If your school has its own newsletter or magazine, volunteer to do some writing. If there isn't one, get some friends together and suggest starting one yourself! Why not start a fanzine, or website on whatever gets you going, be it dance music, snowboarding or green issues. Keep an eye out for writing competitions to enter. Many teen mags run talent competitions and broadsheet newspapers run awards for young journalists. The more practice, experience and work you get into print, the better. Write to your local newspaper and ask for some work experience in your vacations or send them some ideas. Write about what interests you. You never know, the local paper could be looking for someone to write TV, music or movie reviews! Or maybe they'd be interested in a teen column.

School qualifications will get you into a course at college, but that won't necessarily land you a job. A university degree in English Literature is not essential. A college course in English, Media Studies or Journalism will be useful, but you don't necessarily need it to get a job on a magazine. Some courses are geared towards newspaper journalism. Speak to your careers advisor for help on choosing a course. Most magazine editors use computer software called Word, but there are many others as well. They need to know a bit of Quark, the package most often used to design a page, which helps them make corrections on screen.

Stay on at school or go to college if you want to carry on studying, but the best thing you can do is get as much work experience as possible. Many editors started out doing stuff for free. Others get jobs as editorial assistants and work their way up. Write to the editor of a magazine you'd like to work on and ask for a placement. These days, 'workies' can be anything from 14 to 25 years old. Offer to make coffee and don't expect to be writing on the first day. Be enthusiastic, don't be cocky and you'll learn loads about how a magazine is run and the jobs everybody does. More importantly, you'll have made some contacts that you can use in the future.

"When I left college I did work experience on a teen magazine for three months. I may have been poor but it was worth it. I learned loads of computer skills. I had to open the mail and do a bit of filing, but I did the cool stuff, too. I helped the editor on photo shoots with TV presenters and pop stars and sometimes she took me to see new bands and films in the evenings. I wrote a feature on environmental issues, which is a great start for my portfolio. Now I have work in print and a contacts book that's good enough to go for a paid job!"

RACHEL ASHCROFT, 21

Job Description

Isn't it all schmoozing with stars and doing lunch all day? Er, no such luck. Most editors rarely get time for fun! They lead features meetings for each issue to decide what's going in the mag. They assign writers to each feature and secure personalities for cover stories and interviews. Then they put together a flat plan, which shows what's in the mag, page by page. Editors read and edit all the copy and then it goes to the designer to lay out. An editor is also responsible for recruiting, liaising with the advertising

MAGAZINE EDITOR

team and keeping an eye on the monthly budget. Reading other press mags and keeping ahead of the competition is important. Then there's the whole team to look out for!

My Big Break

"At fifteen, I was entering writing competitions and winning one a year. Empire was my favorite magazine so I wrote to the editor with a list of ten feature ideas. He commissioned one on the Top 10 Brainy Stars in the film industry. I actually trained to be a doctor."

EMMA COCHRANE, EDITOR OF EMPIRE, UK

Do's and Don't's

Magazine publishing is highly competitive, so make sure you stand out from the crowd!

Do: Get work experience on a magazine or area that interests you or at the publishing company you'd like to work for. Even if you're not placed on your kind of mag, at least the company will know your name. Your foot's in the door so get noticed!

Do: Send in samples of your writing and a list of original feature ideas that no magazine has thought of before. Know the magazine and its readership and identify what you can offer it.

Do: Make sure you send ideas and samples to the right

person. The features editor commissions a lot of features, but both the editor and the features editor look out for new talent.

Do: Make personal contact. Try to set up an appointment with the editor or features editor. (Editors are extremely busy so be enthusiastic but don't stalk them!) It doesn't matter if there is no job available. You can ask about the industry, their jobs and show them your ideas. Talk to people and they will remember you.

Do: Write to them every month with some ideas, or, if you've got one, send them your website address.

Do: Keep your cover letter and CV to one page. Type them out, use decent paper and make sure you address it to the right person. Applications that are well presented and a bit original don't get thrown in the trash!

Do: Put your most relevant experience at the top of your CV. If you have none, make the experience you do have as relevant as possible to the job you're going for. Say what your role and skills were that show your initiative, ability to come up with ideas and be a good team player. The fact that you've held down a job and been responsible is a good start.

Do: Look for inspiration around you, whether it's TV, movies, fashion or the people you meet. You need to be in touch and on the ball.

Don't: Use silly gimmicks to get noticed. Don't send a photo (they're interested in what you write, not what you look like), don't write Sir or Madam and don't send a photocopied letter with the name changed at the top.

Don't: Act as if you're too good to do a job when you're on work experience. Offer to help, be friendly to everyone and be on time.

Don't: Give up or listen to people who say you can't do it. If it's not been done before, you can be the first!

"I was told that I would never be an editor, just a deputy editor, by someone working in men's magazines. I bit my tongue and proved that I could do it."

Emma Cochrane edited Total Film from 1997-1999, whose readers are 83 percent male and is now the editor of Empire, whose readers are 70 percent male.

Why Being a Magazine Editor can be a Fairytale

"I get to travel a lot and see loads of films before they come out. It's not necessarily about the stars. Meeting the people working behind the scenes on movie sets is really interesting. The best movie star I interviewed is Will Smith. He's really funny and bright. He's also really polite. No matter how many interviews he's done, he makes everyone feel really special."

EMMA COCHRANE, EDITOR OF EMPIRE, UK

Why Being a Magazine Editor can be a Nightmare

"Deadlines can be tight and relentless. On press day, and up against it, I've still been at my desk at 2 a.m. and back in by 7 a.m. the next morning. Then, just when you think you've put an issue to bed and you can relax, a big news story breaks – and you have to start over. But this is actually one of the best jobs ever...and I have to talk about the bad parts!"

KITTY MELROSE, EDITOR OF T2, THE TEEN SECTION OF THE SUNDAY TELEGRAPH

Hours

Be prepared to work long hours and give up your own time to go to launches, film screenings or gigs in the evenings. OK, it does sound pretty fun, but it can interfere with your social life. (Hey! Where did that boyfriend go?!) To get ahead, you have to live your magazine. Editors rarely switch off at 5.30 p.m. on a Friday. If they're not still in the office making sure the deadlines are met, they're keeping an eye out for new ideas 24/7!

"If I'm still in the office at 11 p.m., at least I know the piece I'm editing will flow better for the reader."

LAURA LEE DAVIES, EDITOR OF TIME OUT, LONDON

MAGAZINE EDITOR

Salary

An editor of a children's or teen magazine can earn anything between £25,000 and £35,000 ($37,500 and $52,500). The editor of a major global title, such as Vogue, can earn anything between £70,000 and £150,000 ($105,000 and $225,000). There have been some great success stories in publishing and if your magazine hits a market at the right time, it can make you millions.

Perks and Pitfalls

It gets tough at the top but the little things make it all worthwhile!

Perk: Variety! The pace is so fast and every day is different, so you'll never get bored. (Exhausted, maybe . . . but, never bored!)

Perk: If you're editing an entertainment magazine, you can interview all the people that interest you, whether it's Josh Hartnett, Sophia Coppola or Hilary Clinton!

Perk: You may be asked to represent the magazine and its readers on radio, TV or the internet.

Perk: The freebies! From film tickets, videos and CD's to books, toys, and invitations, your mailbox will be chocca!

Perk: Realize your creative streak. Your decision is final and what you say, goes!

Perk: You can use your ideas to make a difference and give your readers entertainment and inspiration, a mag that challenges them and a mag that really matters!

"There's a more sophisticated teenager out there who's interested in more than what I call the three B's – Boys, Beauty and Bodies. We wanted to start a smarter magazine that deals with real girls and the real issues they face today. A lot of magazines are replicas of one another and we try to be different. We don't glorify manufactured boy bands. When we put Britney on the cover our readers complained and said, 'She's bubblegum, she has fake breasts. We're smarter than that.' And we don't run posters because our readers would be offended, quite frankly."

LAURI BERGER, EDITOR IN CHIEF, JUMP, US

Pitfall: Long hours. Constant deadlines mean this is no 9 – 5 job.

Pitfall: Creative types might find the commercial side a bit of a drag – especially all those meetings with the advertising team.

Pitfall: If something goes wrong, you've got to take responsibility – even if it's not your fault.

Pitfall: Keeping your team motivated – and in check! – means you must be aware of everybody's needs, not just your own!

Pitfall: You may have to compromise your strong ideas. The bottom line is you have to sell copies.

MAGAZINE EDITOR

Other Careers in Magazine Publishing

There are heaps of interesting jobs in magazines, or consumer journalism. Many editors started out as editorial assistants, which involves giving editorial support to the features team, the deputy editor and the editor. Some art editors, the people who design the magazine, go on to become editors. (An editor is a manager who can spot a good story and visualize it, too.) To become a designer or an art editor, you'll need to do a course in graphic design.

Lots of writers aim to become feature editors because it means having a big say in the content of the magazine and who writes it without the responsibility of managing the whole team.

If you like the idea of being your own boss and writing for different magazines, you can be a freelance writer. This gives you more freedom, but less job stability and no holiday or sick pay. Freelance writers aren't paid a salary by one employer – they're paid at different times by different people, so they need to be clued up to their money matters. The best way to start is to send copies of your work to the magazine you'd like to write for. Call up first and find out who commissions new writers. Ask to speak to them and tell them you'll be sending some examples of your work. Follow up your first call after two or three days to make sure they have received it. Calling up and making personal contact means you're more likely to be remembered. But don't be a stalker – magazine staff are madly busy! There are courses for freelance writing – you'll see them advertised in the media job sections of newspapers. However, doing work experience will teach you a whole lot more about what really goes on. More importantly, you can schmooze with the person who does the commissioning!

For those of you with a good eye for detail and an interest in photography, being a picture editor could be up your street. Picture editors choose photographs from picture agencies, select photographers and models, find locations for shoots and help the art editor direct the photo shoots.

Many magazine editors are now crossing over into Web journalism. This requires a higher degree of computer literacy and the pace of news is much faster. However, the possibilities for more interactive features are huge.

And if you're a persuasive type, copy writing might be for you. Copy writers write to sell a product and are needed everywhere from advertising agencies and record companies to a computer games website.

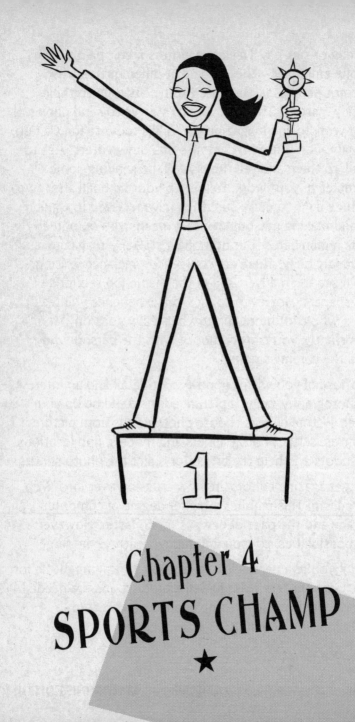

Chapter 4
SPORTS CHAMP

★

Sports Champ

The suspense, the adrenaline, the competition, the team spirit, the action, the thrills, the roar of the crowd, the rising power of your body, the buzz – and yes, close your eyes and imagine – the glory of winning! If you get a real kick out of sports, (and, no, I'm not talking about from your couch), if there are sports you just can't wait to play every week, then why not think about making it your future?

If you are much happier on the playing field than in that stuffy old classroom, feel your most challenged and happiest when you're active, and – this bit's pretty important – you're rather excellent at sports, then start believing and go for it!

Glam Factor	5
Brain Factor	2
Travel Factor	5
Money Factor	5
Stability Factor	2

Have I Got the Right Personality for the Job?

Having natural talent is just the beginning. Whatever your sport, the strength of your mind is as vital as the strength of your body. Mind and body work together, like, well like, Dawson and Joey, Marge and Homer or Mulder and Scully. Every sportsperson has a fit and healthy body but it is confidence, determination and belief in themselves that make them go the distance. For the professionals, a disciplined attitude of mind is everything.

"I don't believe that we're arrogant, but in professional sports it's a bad thing if you believe that someone else is better than you. I believe I'm the best. It takes up more energy being negative. I prefer to surround myself with positive thoughts. It's how I've always been, it's something my parents taught me."

TENNIS STAR, VENUS WILLIAMS, EXPLAINS WHY SHE'S NOT SHORT ON CONFIDENCE!

Sports can involve a lot of pressure, so you need to be mature and level-headed. If things go wrong and you don't progress as fast as you want, you've got to deal with it and get on with it. Stamina, a competitive spirit, staying positive, loving what you do and wanting to succeed are all important.

"To be successful you need to have a lot of heart, determination and always believe that there is room for improvement in your game. Always work hard, put in the extra time it takes to be the best, have a positive attitude and be a good listener. Always remember that ATTITUDE IS EVERYTHING."

LISA LESLIE, 28, LA SPARKS, WNBA

"I am quite a laid-back character, but there are other players who are completely different. You just need to be your own person and be prepared to work hard at your game."

HANNAH COLLIN, 18, TENNIS PLAYER AND NATIONAL SINGLES CHAMPION

Did You Know?

Venus Williams started playing tennis aged four. Serena, her sister, started when she was five. Both turned pro at 14.

Getting Started

"I tried everything when I was younger, and I loved skating the most. Every day I wanted to do it more and more. That's how you know you want to do something."

TARA LIPINSKI, YOUNGEST FIGURE SKATER TO WIN OLYMPIC GOLD

If your sport is not played at your school or college, talk to your PE teacher about introducing it. Get some like-minded friends together to show there's plenty of interest. If your school makes the excuse that none of the staff play it, then suggest they get someone in, who can, even if it's for just one lunch hour a week!

"I was fifteen when I started playing basketball and it wasn't really very popular then. Our school didn't even have nets or a full court so we had to play in the gym."

ANDREA CONGREAVES, 30, WNBA

If you're playing a team sport like football, join a local league or a Saturday league.

"Start by looking for little leagues – that's where most women's clubs do their scouting. From that club, you can be picked to play for your county, then for your country!"

BETH SIMM, 16, 1ST TEAM, WIMBLEDON LADIES FOOTBALL CLUB

If you haven't already tried your local sports center, check out their notice board and ask about local clubs and teams you can join. They should also be able to tell you about mini camps, tournaments or other opportunities. The main thing is to stay active in your sport and be committed to your training. Create good habits and your skills will improve. You have to be your own coach, too!

Don't forget, sport is about fun, too, and you shouldn't let it take over you life.

> *"When you're young, stay open minded. Don't tie yourself down to one thing too early. Don't limit yourself to one sport."*
>
> JESS GARLAND, 20, CAPTAIN OF U21's ENGLAND NETBALL SQUAD

There's no one route to making a career out of sports and fitness. From apprenticeships and traineeships, to college courses, every sports champ comes from a different background. Passing English, mathematics and science exams is important if you're thinking about going into further education to study a course such as Physical Education, Sports Science, Nutrition, Sports and Recreation Management (Coaching), or Leisure Studies.

My Big Break

"I hated school and everyone in it. All my friends had left and I was studying to go to university. I wasn't sure what degree course I wanted to do. I thought about English and I thought about being a TV Presenter, too. I decided to drop out and travel for a year and I told my mum I'd go back to school the next year. I went on the ferry to France and ended up in the Alps. I stayed in the cheapest hotels

 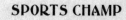

and eventually got a job cleaning the chalets. They helped me get a lift pass, snowboard and all the gear. I progressed very quickly, so I didn't want to give it up. I went home for one summer and went back to the Alps for the winter. This time, I got an apartment, sharing with lots of other snowboarders. It was so cramped and I wasn't earning much money but I put up with it because I wanted to snowboard. I got good enough to enter the British Championships and won the Big Air. Afterwards, I was approached by a management company and got my first sponsor!"

Melanie Leando, 24, snowboarder and British Big Air champion, has never taken a snowboarding lesson in her life. She learned all the basics from friends and learned everything else from watching others.

Do's and Don't's

Do: Get your education and have other interests and skills. A career as a professional sportsperson is limited. You won't be as fast and agile when you're 35!

"If I hadn't been a tennis player, I would like to have been a fashion designer. I am starting fashion design lessons this autumn and this is the direction I would like to move into when my tennis career is eventually over."

TENNIS ACE, SERENA WILLIAMS, IS MAKING PLANS ALREADY!

> *"I'm going to college to study PE, English and Biology. I want to learn how to coach football so I can be a part of it always."*
>
> BETH SIMM, 16, 1ST TEAM, WIMBLEDON LADIES FOOTBALL CLUB

Do: Listen to advice from people you respect and be prepared to make sacrifices. If you haven't got much family support, talk to instructors at school or your local club for advice.

Do: Be aware that there will be obstacles and drawbacks and, at worst, discrimination, particularly if your sport is traditionally seen as a men's sport. You'll probably find these will make you all the more determined!

Do: Be careful who you associate with and be wary of people who may try to exploit you, by offering you steroids, for example.

Do: Keep focusing on your goal and when things get tough, just think about your dream!

Don't: Listen to anyone who says you can't do it because you're a girl. You can do anything you like.

Don't: Accept drugs from anyone. Testing for use of steroids and other drugs is carried out before all major competitions. Those that use them are booted out.

SPORTS CHAMP

Why Being a Sports Champ can be a Fairytale

"Going to the Commonwealth Games in Qualalumpa in 1998 was amazing. We were there for a month earlier in the year and then for another month during the Games. All the famous British athletes were there, like Colin Jackson and Denise Lewis. It was fantastic to watch other athletes, to see them train and perform, to see how they live their sport."

OLIVIA MURPHY, 23, ENGLAND NETBALL CAPTAIN

Why Being a Sports Champ can be a Nightmare

"I'd like to forget the time I fractured my foot. We were getting ready for the European Championships. It was the quarterfinal and I was out! I don't remember how I did it, it wasn't on court. But when I put my foot down the pain was excruciating! I walked in the locker room and the whole emotion just dropped. It was really hard to see them lose their momentum. They needed me and I had to sit on the bench and watch! It was so frustrating!

ANDREA CONGREAVES, WNBA

Hours

As a career, sports take up a lot of your life. You have to give it 100 percent and that can mean training and touring for nine months out of the year – without a break. You have to be prepared to see less of your family and friends and your social life has to take a back seat.

Britain's number one gymnast, eighteen-year old Lisa Mason, has put everything on hold – including college! – to prepare for the qualifiers for the Sydney Olympics. She trains seven hours a day, six days a week.

"It is very demanding," says Lisa, "and I spend lots of time away from my family, but it's not forever. I just want to go to Sydney and do my best."

Salary

Some young sports stars are lucky enough to get a Lottery grant or sponsorship. If a company wants to sponsor you, they will pay all your expenses and supply you with free clothes and equipment. In return, you have to promote their product. For example, if you were being photographed for a newspaper, you'd have to wear all their clothes and make sure all the logos were totally visible.

> *Sally Gunnell OBE is the UK's greatest female athlete, ever. She is the only woman in history to have held, simultaneously, all four gold medals – Olympic, World, Commonwealth and European.*

Sportspeople have the potential to make a lot of money. A new player in the WNBA can earn $30,000 (£20,000) a year. Six to eight years later that could rise to $90,000 (£60,000) a year. They can be offered millions to do global advertising campaigns for brands like Nike and Reebok.

Perks and Pitfalls

"The best part about my job is having the opportunity to make people happy, to touch a lot of peoples' lives in a positive way – and to be able to tell my story in the hope that it will encourage others to aspire to reach their dreams. The worst part about my job is all of the flying we have to do. I don't like to fly."

Even WNBA star, Lisa Leslie, has to do stuff she hates!

Perk: The team spirit! Sport is very confidence building and playing in a team provides a support network, just like a second family.

Perk: The opportunities to travel are coooool!

"I can't wait for the World Youth Championships Tour to Australia and the Caribbean. You're there with all the players you know and captaining the side is an honor. I've already been to Australia twice and some people never go in a lifetime."

JESS GARLAND, 20, U21's ENGLAND NETBALL SQUAD

Perk: Representing your school, club, county or country is something to be proud of.

Perk: Taking part in prestigious competitions.

Perk: If you're sponsored, funded or professional, you get paid for doing what you love!

"I'm sponsored by Casio, G Shock, Oakley and Nokia, so I get free watches, shades and phones. All my snowboarding equipment is free because Salomon sponsors me, too – plus I get lots of free street gear. I'm also sponsored by Thompson, who supply flights, vacation and lift passes."

MELANIE LEANDO, 24, CHAMPION SNOWBOARDER

Perk: Winning! Medals, prize money, adoration, the recognition and the fame! Winning is fun!

Pitfall: Training and touring can be gruelling and take you away from family and friends for long periods.

Pitfall: The injuries and the pressure! Your body and mind take a bruisin'.

"It can be tough. There have been days when I've felt like giving in … then I'd tell myself, 'I have my heart, my soul, my mind – but my body's a little bit messed up.' It helps having my dog and positive people around!"

ALPINE SKIER, PICABO STREET – SUPER-G GOLD MEDALIST

 SPORTS CHAMP

> "The run lasts a minute and a half so I can't stand there worrying about how good the person in front is. It's like ice-skating in that it's really easy to make a mistake. That's why you have to learn to compete against yourself and do your very best on the day."
>
> CHAMPION SNOWBOARDER, MELANIE LEANDO, ON THE PRESSURE OF THE HALF-PIPE

Pitfall: In some sports, such as football, women are still given a back seat to men, in terms of funding and facilities.

> "I played football with the boys at home. I didn't realize until I actually went to school that I wouldn't be allowed to play it there. When I was younger, we got kicked out of our training hall so the boys could use it."
>
> CARRIE BASSETT, 27, WIMBLEDON LADIES FOOTBALL CLUB

Pitfall: You've got to eat healthy, like, ALL the time. So there's no midnight feasting on chocolate, cakes and other yummy treats before a competition. Boring.

Pitfall: Losing. Damn!

◎ Tip from the Top ◎

Take a tip from teen tennis star, Venus Williams, who says her ambition is, "To do everything that I want to do in life and to not be afraid to try anything, even if I fail."

Did You Know?

Venus Williams' serve has been timed at 117 miles per hour.

Other Careers in Sports

There are millions of people working in the sport and fitness industry. Some of them support full time professionals, such as physiotherapists and coaches. Many work with amateurs and the general public, such as fitness instructors, lifeguards, PE teachers and personal trainers. You may not be aware of all these: nutritionist, referee, sports agent, sports PR, dance teacher, aerobics instructor, yoga teacher, martial arts instructor, snowboarding instructor, sports commentator or presenter, leisure center manager, leisure attendant, outdoor education instructor, masseur, groundsperson. And how about, stuntperson?!

Behind every triumph, glory and magic moment, there's a lot of hard work and sweat! Like any glamorous profession, it's easy to **IMAGINE** being a sports champ. The question is, do you have the personality, ambition, belief in yourself and dedication to hard work that's necessary to actually see if you can make a career of it? There's some luck involved, too, not just skill (though you need **PLENTY** of that!). You have to be in the right place at the right time and the right person has to notice you. And remember: competitive sports careers are short-lived and everybody has to make a living. So, if you love sports so much you can't imagine life without them, then develop your qualifications to support yourself in a related sports career. And, at the same time, you can put your heart and soul into trying to be the new, world champion of your chosen sport!

SPORTS CHAMP

Chapter 5
SUPERMODEL
★

Supermodel

Would you love a job that sends you all over the world, from Tokyo one day to a tropical beach the next? Would you get a kick out of wearing designer clothes, having a stack of invitations to showbiz parties and meeting loads of famous people?

Everywhere you look there's a beautiful girl smiling back at you. She's in magazines, on billboards, on TV commercials, and she seems perfect! It's no wonder so many girls dream about being a model. Are you one of them? If you dream about strutting your stuff on the catwalk with the likes of Kate, Naomi and Gisele, listen up!

Modeling isn't just about swaying those hips down the catwalk and it takes more than a pretty face to succeed in this business. Modeling is highly competitive and very few girls make a career out of it. A thick skin, a head for business and lots and lots of confidence are all part of the job. Being a supermodel may look glam but you've gotta be a tough cookie to make it!

If you are photogenic, you don't necessarily need to fit the "pretty" stereotype. You can still do commercial modeling because the demand for models with real character is growing.

> *"Not everyone wants that chocolate box look. You can be a bit chubby, have loads of freckles and slightly goofy teeth; the important thing is to look healthy. Nickelodeon recently called us and asked for a model with braces on her teeth."*
>
> HEATHER MORTON, HEAD OF THE CHILDREN'S MODEL AGENCY, BUBBLEGUM

Open a style magazine and you'll see girls who, not long ago, would have been considered geeky or strange; other-worldly girls and even the girl next door! Funky and quirky is currently where it's at. If you're lucky enough to have the look of the moment (which, I must add, can change in a minute) then you'll be flooded with offers from style mags. But, because the "look of the moment" changes so quickly, your success may be very short lived.

Most catwalk models are freakishly tall and skinny and they are a tiny minority of the many body types that are natural to girls. You've got to be naturally very thin and have longer legs than anyone you've ever met before to consider doing catwalk. To be a model you need to be at least 5 ft

8 inches (1.73cm) tall and measure 34-24-34 inches (86cm-61cm-86cm). For the catwalks of New York, Paris and Milan, models need to be at least 5ft 9 inches tall.

"I hope I'm showing other teenage girls that you don't have to be tall and skinny to be successful. I look at girls on the bus and think, 'you could be doing what I'm doing.'"

Jo Bettany, 19, is a size 14 commercial model who is challenging beauty stereotypes.

Glam Factor	5
Brain Factor	3
Travel Factor	5
Money Factor	5
Stability Factor	0

Have I Got the Right Personality for the Job?

You might be surprised to learn that personality plays a big part in being a top model. You might have the face of an angel and the body of a Barbie doll, but if you can't speak up for yourself, you'll go nowhere. Being a little bit shy is OK when you start out because your confidence will get a real boost with your first modeling job.

"Modeling is a really difficult job. You need to be really thick skinned and strong as there's a lot of rejection. A good model is patient, punctual, organized, dedicated, interesting and out-going. You need to be able to move naturally in front of the camera."

ANGUS MUNRO, HEAD OF FUTURE AT
PREMIER MODEL MANAGEMENT.

"I think I'm a good model because I'm very patient. I did this ad where I had to get down on my knees and hold up this heavy roll of wallpaper. My arm was aching like mad and my knees were killing me and they kept reshooting it! You've got to enjoy it. If you complain you'll get chucked out!"

CARLI HARRIS, 12, MODEL

Getting started

OK, so you've decided to give modeling a try. Think about it very carefully and don't expect miracles overnight. Most importantly, get your education because like any career where you're counting on more than talent, one where you also need luck to get discovered, you'll need a way to make your living until you know if you're going to succeed or not. And anyway, a model's career is usually over well before she is 30. So, if you've had some success, but you haven't managed to make it big time, you'll still need a career that will suit you once modeling is over.

There are a number of ways of getting spotted by a model scout. Hanging out at massive fashion stores is one of them. Going to huge fashion events is another. However, hundreds of wannabe models go to these events in the hope of being spotted so the competition is fierce. Don't bother sending your picture to a fashion magazine; they book models through the agencies. However, keep a look out for modeling competitions in the teen mags.

SUPERMODEL

The traditional route is to send some photographs of yourself to model agencies. Don't waste money getting a professional photographer to take the shots. And if a photographer approaches you and promises to make you a model, don't agree to anything until you've talked to one of your parents first. The photographer may be trying to take advantage of you. You really don't need a portfolio at this stage, anyway. The agency will probably think that even professional shots are below their standard and they'll get their own done. All you need is two decent pictures: a head and shoulders shot and a full-length body shot. So long as you're in focus and there's no zit on the end of your nose, plain old snaps are good enough.

Your next move is to visit your local librarian. She or he can help you find the information you need to contact a professional model's association. Ask the association for a leaflet with their list of approved agencies and phone numbers. Don't bother with any agency that isn't on the professional organization's list because they're likely to be amateurs. And, never answer an advertisement as they are usually from dishonest people who can be very dangerous.

Send your snap shots, with your name and number on the back, to the agencies, but remember that they get up to a 100 photos of gorgeous girls each week and only a tiny handful are selected this way. It's worth calling the agencies to find out if they run regular castings and make an appointment to go in. If you find that the first few agencies turn you away, don't lose heart. Different agencies want different looks. Ask them why you're not suitable and whether they can recommend an agency that might be interested.

Be prepared for an agency to say you are not thin or toned enough. This does not mean that you are overweight or need to diet, it just means you don't fit their criteria. In that case, ask which agencies might be looking for 'real girl' images. Most models are required to be incredibly thin and their weight is below the average

Amazing but true! Top models in Paris learn all their tricks of the trade from a man called J Alexander. The six-foot tall skirt specialist wears high heels and wraps himself in a sheet to show models how to walk in different types of skirt.

of all but a few girls. That's why, unless you're opting for the newer 'real girl' niche, you must be naturally skinny. You simply won't be able to diet down to an extremely low weight without putting your health seriously at risk.

If an agent does take you on, they become what's called your "Mother Agent." They will take photographs of you and start to build your portfolio. Take your mother or a friend to the shoot and don't be afraid to ask questions. Be as proactive and enthusiastic as you can.

The job interview or the "casting" is a tough but important part of modeling. Going to appointments requires dedication and punctuality and leaving them without a job can make you feel worthless and lonely. So, remember: never take a job rejection personally. It just means that you didn't happen to fit that client's criteria for that particular job. Pick yourself up and remind yourself that you did well to make the casting.

There are schools and courses where you can learn to walk the catwalk and do your hair and make-up. Don't bother with them. A good agency will teach you everything you need to know. Many get professional make-up artists and ex-models in to show you how to make the most of your looks.

My Big Break

"I was a real ugly duckling at school. I had short, ginger hair and I thought I was a bit chubby. I'd go into shops and they'd say, 'What do you want young lad?!' Then my mum and Gran entered my picture in a local beauty contest. I knew nothing about it until the local paper ran a huge picture of me! I was 16.

"I didn't win the competition but I got down to the last ten. The competition photographer asked me if I'd thought of modeling and offered me a test. I'd read so many horror stories about sleazy photographers so I said only if I could bring my mum.

"We went to London for the first time and I had my hair and make-up done and my eyebrows plucked. I couldn't believe it was me! I was just a jeans and T-shirt kind of girl. The photographer took the shots to a couple of agencies and one of them took me on!"

REBECCA MADER, 22, MODEL

Do's and Don'ts

Do: Make sure every agency you approach is professional and well-known.

Do: Phone the agencies and make an appointment before you go in.

Do: Get your education. Models are self-employed and manage their own finances so you've got to be smart and savvy, too!

Do: Take a parent or an adult you trust to every casting and job. This is especially important for jobs abroad. You might be streetwise but coping in a foreign country is more difficult than you think. Beware of immoral senior figures who may ask you out or offer you drugs. Don't be flattered; they try it with every new face.

Do: Keep your feet on the ground. The fashion world is a fickle bubble that just isn't real life. Keep in touch with your family and friends and don't lose track of your roots.

Don't: Take a job rejection personally. Remember if your looks don't fit the client's needs, it doesn't mean you're not a gorgeous hip chick!

Don't: Complain or do a job half-heartedly. The client won't ask you back.

Don't: Stand for pushy moms. If your mother has a habit of answering questions for you, explain to her that you need to do the talking or she'll ruin your chances at a casting.

Don't: Obsess about your weight. Unless you're naturally skinny, go for 'real girl, character' modeling or aim for a different fashion career. Dieting will make you miserable and sickly and that's no fun at all!

Don't: Treat modeling like one big party. Don't stay out late, don't do drugs and don't get drunk. Besides ruining your looks, you might end up doing things you'd rather not. Treat it like a business if you want to be taken seriously.

Why Modeling can be a Fairytale

"The best job I've done was a fashion shoot for Looks magazine. They took me to the island of Zanzibar, off the coast of Africa, for ten days. We stayed in really posh hotels and everybody from the magazine was really nice. There were mud huts all over the island. It was just like paradise."

HELEN STINTON, 18, MODEL

Why Modeling can be a Nightmare

"I'll never forget the television commercial I did for Kraft cheese. The idea was that I was on a magic carpet, so I was rigged up in a harness to make it look like I was flying. The special effects man who was controlling the carpet pressed the wrong button. All of a sudden I was hanging up side down, really high up!"

Hours and Salary

Children need a licence to model. Generally, if you're under 16, the number of hours you can work is up to your parents, your school and the local education welfare officer. Ten to fourteen year olds can earn up to £60 or $90 an hour, but magazine work can fall to as low as £35 or $55 an hour. A day's work can pay around £165 or $250 for a magazine shoot and up to £300 or $450 for a commercial job.

"If you're in a TV commercial that gets shown in other countries, you can earn a lot. One girl got £175 (or $266) for a day's shoot and then she was paid £4,000 (or $6080) as a buy-out fee so it can be shown all over the world."

HEATHER MORTON, HEAD OF
CHILDREN'S MODEL AGENCY, BUBBLEGUM

Perks and Pitfalls

Perk: You get to wear loads of cool designer clothes and, if you're lucky, keep them!

Perk: Getting your hair and make-up done and being transformed by top stylists is just another part of the daily routine!

Perk: It gives you loads of new experiences, from meeting famous people to traveling the globe!

Perk: You can earn a pretty penny just by looking pretty (AND working hard, being smart and savvy . . .).

Perk: Modeling opens lots of doors and gives you loads of exposure. It's a great stepping stone to a career in acting, singing or presenting. Cameron Diaz, Cindy Crawford and Milla Jovovich have all made the crossover from modeling into movies!

Pitfall: You never know when your next job is coming.

Pitfall: You'll spend a lot of time away from family and friends and miss out on their fun!

Pitfall: If you're in a monster mood and fed up, you can't let it show. It's your job to turn on the charm and smile, baby!

Pitfall: You have to be prepared to get up early, wait around doing nothing and work long hours.

Pitfall: Shoots aren't always in Paris or on Caribbean beaches. Some clients will reshoot again and again in very cold, dreary conditions (and you may be in swimwear!).

Pitfall: You are constantly being judged on your looks alone and other models can get really competitive and unkind.

Short Cut to the Top

I'm afraid there aren't any, sisters! Turn up to castings on time, work really hard, be proactive and make sure your agency knows how dedicated you are. Don't be a crazy party girl. Cindy Crawford is a businesswoman. The only way to rise to the top is to be professional and give it 100 percent!

☺ Tip from the Top ☺

"Never lose hold of your dream. To be successful you need to be yourself. That's what people are drawn to."

REBECCA MADER, 22, MODEL

Other Careers in the Fashion Business

You don't have to be a supermodel to have all the fun! There are loads of funky jobs in the fashion business. Being a Model Booker, a Model Scout or a model's Personal Assistant will give you access to the glam life.

> "When I was Karen Mulder's PA, I was treated like a princess. We stayed in some amazing places and when she presented the MTV awards, all the celebs popped in to her dressing room. Another time, Karen was recording a single and I had a peep at Geri Halliwell in the studio next door!"

STEPHANIE PIERRE, PREMIER MODEL MANAGEMENT

Or you could be a make-up artist, a stylist, a hairdresser, a fashion designer, a pattern cutter, a photographer, a set designer, a picture editor, or a beauty editor or a fashion editor. A fashion editor chooses all the clothes, models and locations for a shoot and then goes along to help direct it!

There are loads of courses in fashion design and fashion and beauty journalism. The best thing to do is write to request a work experience placement with someone doing the job already. It's the best way to find out what the job really involves!

Children's Model Agencies take on all kinds of girls, of all shapes and sizes. But it's a different story once you hit your late teens. If you're not naturally very thin or stereotypically pretty, there are plus size agencies and character agencies that take on real girls. You're still gorgeous! Remember: If it's not fun, and it doesn't make you feel good about yourself, it ain't worth it!

SUPERMODEL

Chapter 6
FAMOUS AUTHOR

★

Famous Author

A lot of us girls have a natural talent for writing. Well, we're a talented bunch aren't we? Whether we're writing stories and essays at school, letters and emails to our buds or keeping a diary, it can fire up our imaginations, give us a good giggle or be just plain relaxing. Becoming an author isn't something schools tell us we can do. Well, it's not a regular job like teaching is it? But if you're one of those girls who loves her English class (and maybe think about your English teacher a bit too much, too) and find writing rewarding and satisfying, you could make a career out of it. You could write newspaper and magazine articles, write a soap or a film script. You could even write a book. Really. It's that simple. There's just one catch. You're on your own, kiddo.

Glam Factor	4
Brain Factor	5
Travel Factor	1 - 5
Money Factor	5
Stability Factor	3

Fact File

* Academics generally agree that the first-ever novel was written by a woman. Aphra Behn wrote Oroonoko in 1688.

* To become a successful and respected writer, novelist Marian Evans, felt forced to pretend to be a man. She is better known as George Eliot.

Have I Got the Right Personality for the Job?

"If you've got talent, great. But if you've got talent and drive that never stops, you're in with a chance!"

FRANCINE PASCAL, CREATOR OF SWEET VALLEY HIGH AND AUTHOR OF THE FEARLESS SERIES

All authors are very different people. They come from all walks of life. Rich, poor, young, old, silly, different, interesting, and normal; anyone with an imagination can be a writer.

"I used to think I couldn't do it because my life was so boring. I didn't have famous parents or go to amazing places. I was just normal. But every experience is valuable. When you're sweeping the streets or waitressing, you can draw on it later."

JO O'KEEFE, FILM AND TELEVISION SCRIPTWRITER

The one thing writers do have in common is drive and motivation. Lots of people have ideas but if you can't be bothered to put them down, how is anyone going to read them?

To be a success you've got to be disciplined, able to work on your own and set your own targets. Authors work at home alone and make up their own timetable so being well organized and dedicated is crucial. Getting down to work can be difficult if there's no one there nagging you to hurry up and finish!

Getting Started

You don't need training, but many authors start off by writing short stories for newspapers and magazines. Creative writing is a competitive business so get as much practice in as possible. Enter school or magazine fiction writing competitions, write for the school paper or website or send off some ideas, articles or a short story to a children's magazine. Good books are The Writer's Market (UK) and the Hollis Press and PR Guide (US).

They list the names of publishing companies, magazine editors and the kind of work they use. Ask your English teacher for advice and help with your writing and about local creative writing groups you could join. And read all different kinds of writing, novels, poetry, short stories, and magazines for ideas!

You don't need to be superhuman at passing exams to be a writer. However, the important ones to pass are English and History. Staying on at school and going into further education or college isn't vital, but any English, Media, Journalism, Theatre or Communication studies course will be useful.

You're never too young to start writing. Jacqueline Wilson, author of top teen trilogy, Girls In Love, Girls Under Pressure and Girls Out Late, wrote her first book when she was nine! "It was always my ambition to be a writer when I was at school and I always wrote stories. My teachers never told me I was a born writer or anything like that, though, and my parents thought I was mad!"

Harry Potter creator, JK Rowling, always wanted to be a writer, too and wrote her first book, called Rabbit, at the age of six! "Ever since Rabbit and his friend, Miss Bee, I have wanted to be a writer, though I rarely told anyone

FAMOUS AUTHOR

so. I was so afraid they'd tell me I didn't have a hope. I wrote a lot in my teens, but I never showed any of it to my friends, except for funny stories that featured us all as thinly disguised characters."

My Big Break

To get your story published, you'll need to send a synopsis (a short description of the story or subject) and two or three chapters to a literary agent. You can find their addresses in The Writer's and Artist's Yearbook and other similar industry publications. It also gives you tips on how to present and send your story, or manuscript. Your library and good bookshops should be able to help you locate these books.

"I left school at 17 and gave up. I was doing English, Art and Drama. It wasn't the stress, I just didn't like school and I wanted to write. My parents were great about it, so long as I was doing something positive and creative. I joined a creative writing course in the evenings and started writing a book. I wanted to write about adolescence, something raw, of the era, written by a teen.

"I was working from 8 a.m. till 6 p.m. so it was quite intensive. After three or four months I was half way through the book and sent it to two agents. One phoned up at 8.55 a.m. on a Monday morning and said he wanted to represent me and that we should find a publisher."

Within weeks, Rebecca Ray, had two major publishing houses bidding for her first book, A Certain Age. It took six months to write.

93   **FAMOUS AUTHOR**

Do's and Don't's

Do: Practice writing! Whether it's keeping a diary or emailing friends, get into the habit of writing. Writing is a competitive field, so keep it as a hobby, even if you're not getting work in print.

Do: Write about stuff you know, be it school, your Saturday job, your family, youth club or a top night out. Write about what happens to you, your thoughts and your feelings.

> "If it feels good and easy to write, if the words are flowing off the page, you're writing about the right thing. If you're finding it difficult, think of something else. I've tried loads of ideas and given them up."
>
> REBECCA RAY

Do: Sell yourself! Send your story or manuscript to one or two agents, or publishers. Agents represent lots of different writers and help them find a suitable publisher. Get some feedback from one or two, but you don't need to go to the trouble of sending it to fifty (at least, not all at once)!

Do: Be prepared for rejection. Agents have mountains of manuscripts to read and even the best writers experience set-backs.

Do: Be persistent, disciplined and work hard. If it's meant to be, it will happen!

Don't: Give up just because you're not academically great or don't have formal qualifications. Great writers are not always from academic backgrounds.

Don't: Ignore any aspect of your life, even if you think it's boring.

Don't: Listen to parents or teachers who tell you can't do it. If you love writing, you can seek advise elsewhere. Join a local writing group and write to your favorite author via their publisher or website.

"I hated my new school. My new teacher, Mrs Morgan, scared the life out of me. She positioned everyone in the class according to how smart she thought they were; the brightest sat on the left, and everyone she thought was dim sat on her right. I was as far right as you could get without sitting in the playground! "

JK ROWLING

Why Writing can be a Fairytale

"Kids write me letters and I meet readers at book signings. I've really got to know my readers and I still write to pen pals who are now adults and I've known since they were girls. Money from The Babysitter's Club and related products has helped me start a foundation that gives grants to different organizations. Organizations that support children, education, literacy, the homeless and stray animals have all benefited. It's very rewarding."

ANN M MARTIN, AUTHOR OF THE BABYSITTER'S CLUB

FAMOUS AUTHOR

Why Writing can be a Nightmare

When Louise Bagshawe sent in her manuscript for Career Girls, she got a shock. "The editor said I'd lost my sparkle and told me to start again. It was like winning the Lottery, then finding out my ticket wasn't valid. So I bought a pile of blockbusters and started reading. They reminded me of my aim to be a trashy novelist. Once I stopped trying to be so literary, it flowed."

Hours

If you're an author, you make the rules. You still have to meet a deadline so working a bit every day makes sense. Every author has their own pattern that works best for them.

"I'm very disciplined but I don't work weekends and I take a holiday when I want. I write four pages on the computer a day. However long it takes, I write those four pages. If I'm really not in the right mood, I write them anyway. It's as if someone fixes it in the night because they're never so terrible the next morning!"

FRANCINE PASCAL

Some writers work all morning and take the afternoon off, others work from 8 a.m. – 6 p.m., and some even work late at night. It just depends on what works for you. Everyone has a more creative time of day. There's no right or wrong way so long as you get it done! Experiment, and see what works for you. But one thing is sure: whenever it is that you decide to write, you must write, whether you feel like it or not. That's part of the discipline of being a successful writer.

Salary

Louise Bagshawe got a £70,000 ($112,500) two book deal at 23. Her book, Career Girls, was the first of four blockbusters to sell more than 200,000 copies, making her one of the youngest self-made millionaires by the age of 25.

Multi-award winning author JK Rowling has sold more than seven million copies of the three Harry Potter books, as well as film rights to the first two books for "a substantial seven figure sum." Can writing a best seller make you a millionaire? Go figure!

But, Where do the Ideas Come From?

Any life experience, memory or emotion can lead to an idea for a book.

FAMOUS AUTHOR

"As a teenager I wanted to teach because I enjoyed working with kids. I always babysat and worked with kids in the summer and at day camps for children with learning difficulties. Some of the things that happened to me, or friends I knew, when we were babysitting, gave me inspiration as well as my own feelings as a kid."

ANN M MARTIN, AUTHOR OF THE BABYSITTER'S CLUB

"Ten years ago I read a science story in the New York Times about a woman whose body just didn't respond to fear. If someone held a gun to her head, there was no reaction, no adrenaline rush at all. I took it one step further and thought, "What if a girl was born without the fear gene. No one knows if it exists or not. What if a little girl could overmatch all these boys? There aren't enough heroines out there and it's a real girl empowerment time, so Fearless suited this time perfectly."

FRANCINE PASCAL ON HER INSPIRATION FOR GAIA, THE HEROINE OF THE FEARLESS SERIES

"Occasionally I see someone walking along the road who looks interesting, and I might meet a girl with an unusual name when I'm signing books in a school, but mostly I make my characters up. My stories come from my own memories, but I also go to schools and talk to girls about their lives, what's important to them, how late they're allowed to stay out, that kind of thing."

JACQUELINE WILSON GETS INSPIRATION FOR HER TEEN NOVELS

"Sometimes they just come (like magic) and other times I have to sit and think for about a week before I manage to work out how something will happen. Where the idea for Harry Potter actually came from I couldn't tell you. I was traveling on a train between Manchester and London and it just popped into my head. I spent four hours thinking about what Hogwarts would be like. It was the most interesting train journey I've ever taken. By the time I got off at Kings Cross many of the characters in the books had already been invented."

JK ROWLING, ON HER IDEA FOR THE HARRY POTTER SERIES

FAMOUS AUTHOR

> *"I'm not a great ideas person. I just wanted to write about a girl growing away from her family. Adults write most books about adolescence. I was that age, so I felt close to it."*
>
> REBECCA RAY, WHO LEFT SCHOOL AT 16 AND FINISHED HER FIRST BOOK, *A CERTAIN AGE*, AT 17.

Perks and Pitfalls

Perk: Get up when you want, wear what you want, work when you want, write what you want!

Perk: Respect. If you're a success, you'll get recognition. When Louise Bagshawe's book, Career Girls, came out, ads for the book were plastered all over London buses. "My boss, who sacked me, nearly crashed when he saw it, so I've been told!"

Perk: Fortune. If you write a best seller, especially one that will make a good film, let's just say you'll be sorted for pocket money!

Perk: You get to meet lots of creative people and the free lunch invitations from the media will flood in.

Pitfall: Being on your own and motivating yourself to work can be tough and make you feel isolated (cuddly pets come in handy here!).

Pitfall: Long term stress or pressure. Knowing how much work you have to get through can weigh heavily on your mind.

Pitfall: Writer's block. Some days you're just not in the mood. In case of emergency, get down to the gym, go for a swim, or visit a friend (briefly!). If none of those work, just write it anyway and see how it looks in the morning!

Pitfall: There's no money until you get a publisher.

☺ Tip from the Top ☺

"If you get a good idea, get it down right away. There's a chance that five or six other people will have had the same idea, so be the first to start writing!"

FRANCINE PASCAL

Other Careers in Writing and Publishing

If you're good at creative writing, there are loads of possibilities!

You could be a script editor, film or TV scriptwriter, a journalist, a poet, a freelance writer. Lots of magazines run short stories, as well as articles and reviews. A job at a publishing house can involve everything from writing book jackets and press releases to editing material. Get inside the industry and doors will open.

"I got a job as a receptionist at a film company. I kept my mouth shut and my ears open and learned a lot about the film industry. I had no secretarial skills and wrote a script on my computer. A runner there said he knew an agent and passed it on to him."

JO O'KEEFE, TV AND FILM SCRIPT WRITER

FAMOUS AUTHOR

Chapter 7
FIREFIGHTER
★

Firefighter

If you're looking for a job that offers excitement, variety and the opportunity to really help people; a physical job that gets you out into the community and won't tie you to an office desk, then why not consider firefighting? No, seriously. OK, there are obvious risks involved. Your job is to run into a burning building when everyone else is running out! But, with the right attitude and training, you could be saving lives. How's that for job satisfaction! (Just don't mention it to your parents, yet.)

"When I was a kid there was a fire in our street, four doors down. I was so impressed by all the firefighters that the danger didn't occur to me. It doesn't now. But I never thought I'd be able to do it. I just thought, 'I wish girls could do that.'"

PAMELA OPARAOCHA, 32, FIREFIGHTER

Glam Factor	1
Brain Factor	3
Travel Factor	3
Money Factor	3
Stability Factor	5

Have I Got the Right Personality for the Job?

Lets start with courage. You're gonna need it. But don't be scared off yet. After all their training, women firefighters say they can't wait to get out there and tackle their first real fire! If you are calm in a crisis, able to think on your feet, act quickly and have a genuine desire to help and work with others, then you're made of the right stuff. Firefighting is not about heroics. If you're a loner and need to prove yourself, you'll get kicked out, because firefighting is about teamwork. But let's face it: we girls are bigger than that. We don't carry massive egos around and we work well in a team. We're perfect for the job!

Good firefighters are responsible, disciplined and sensitive enough to handle members of the public when they're very distressed. The job is physically and mentally demanding and requires stamina and reliability. But the results are very rewarding. Physical fitness is key to this job. And, you can't be a wuss.

> *"You have to be a strong character. You can't be squeamish because at the very worst, you're gonna see dead bodies that look pretty bad. You're working with mostly men and in the station there's a lot of banter going on so you have to be able to take a joke. But once we're called out, everyone pulls together and looks out for each other. I have great work mates. They're fantastic. I do think men are less competitive with women there."*
>
> DANIELLE COTTON, 31, STATION OFFICER AND HIGHEST RANKING FEMALE FIREFIGHTER IN THE UK

Women's Work

> There are 5,684 firefighters in the London Fire Brigade; 61 are women.
>
> January 2000

Just like the police and the army,
firefighting is traditionally seen as a man's job. Some female firefighters have had problems with their male colleagues; others have not.

"I've been a firefighter for twelve years. After seven years I decided to become an officer (although you can train for this promotion after two years). Now I'm an officer. There have been some who don't like taking orders from me. One guy would just ignore me. He clearly felt threatened. It's fear of change."

DANIELLE COTTON, 31, STATION OFFICER

Fortunately for Danielle, who loves her job madly, this doesn't happen every day. Most Fire Departments are looking to recruit more ethnic minorities and more women, in an effort to fairly represent their community.

"It is important that women do not feel excluded from the fire service. The more that female firefighters are seen by the public, the greater the number of women who will consider the fire service to be the occupation for them"

HOME OFFICE MINISTER, MIKE O'BRIEN

"When I tell people what I do, the men say, 'Can you give us a fireman's lift?' The women ask intelligent questions about what we do and if we ever get hurt. There's always two of you and you've got radio control."

PAMELA OPARAOCHA, 32, FIREFIGHTER

> *"The fire service needs women. It's good to have a physical mixture. Smaller people can get in narrow gaps and small spaces."*
>
> DANIELLE COTTON, 31, FIREFIGHTER

Getting Started

Qualifications really aren't that important. Get a good all-round education, pass your English and Mathematics exams, use common sense and you've got a chance. However, once you've decided you're interested, there are a lot of tests, both the physical and the academic kind, to get through. But don't be put off. The fire service offers a lot of help and support to help you pass them all! You do need to be 18, have perfect eye sight and be fit and active. So go get some exercise, girl!

First you should call your nearest fire department for an information pack, and ask about Open Days. They will give you a good idea of what to expect from the entrance tests and the job itself.

Once your application is accepted, you will need to pass the physical and written tests. The fitness tests are designed to measure strength, stamina and agility. You'll be asked to do all kinds of stuff, from climbing a tower while wearing all the protective clothing and equipment to crawling through a small space with limited vision. Get through these and you'll be asked to do a series of written tests to rate your problem solving skills and how well you'll fit into a team of firefighters.

FIREFIGHTER

If you pass the physical and written tests, you'll be invited to an interview and given a medical and eye examination. You'll also be asked to do more physical tests that are relevant to the job. These will help you decide whether it's the career for you.

One thing you will need is good employment or academic references and a good attendance record. Your sickness record gets the third degree!

Phew! Think it's all over? No such luck, sister! Let the training begin!

Training

Once you've been accepted, you must complete a training course and learn the basic skills of a firefighter. This includes learning first aid and how to use the breathing apparatus, ladders and hoses. You'll also go on drills underground or in a specially created fire house, where gas is used instead of real fire. You're really put through your paces.

"No one knows anything at training school so nobody criticized anyone else. I'm 5ft 10in, but if you're smaller, maybe people would watch to see if you can do it. Your trainers help you a lot."

PAMELA OPARAOCHA, 32,
FIREFIGHTER

Hours

This depends on where you live and what the policy is at your station. At many stations firefighters do shift work. They may work 9 a.m. – 6 p.m. for two days, then for two nights, from 6 p.m. – 9 a.m. Then they take four days off! Shift work can be hard to get used to, but it means there's lots of free time to do other stuff when they are off. They can go to the mall or amusement parks when there's nobody there!

Salary

You won't be buying your parents homes all over the world, but you can earn enough to keep that wardrobe and CD and book collection up to date! And, this is a career with good prospects for promotion.

Perks and Pitfalls

Perk: Helping people, saving lives and dealing with major emergencies is very rewarding. From putting out fires in a home or school to rescuing people trapped in a lift or motorway pile-up, your role is hugely important.

"I rescued a family with four small children who lived above a shop. On one call, we got to a blazing house and two teenage boys were asleep inside. If we hadn't been there, they would have died. That's when I really knew how worthwhile my job is."

DANIELLE COTTON, 31, FIREFIGHTER

FIREFIGHTER

Perk: Excitement, variety and the chance to meet many different people in your community.

Perk: You're working as part of a close-knit team and solving problems while thinking on your feet.

Perk: The hours of work mean there's plenty of time for other interests.

Pitfall: Once you start you are on probation for one to two years. This means you're always being assessed.

Pitfall: You're not always fighting fires or rescuing fluffy animals from trees or tight spots. Some call-outs, called Special Services, deal with flooded premises or chemical spills, making structures safe or clearing a road after a motor accident. You'll also be checking and cleaning equipment at the station or taking part in training exercises.

Pitfall: You've got to be prepared to work outside in all kinds of weather, even when it's wet and cold and you don't know when a job will finish.

Pitfall: Rules. There are quite a few and you must be happy to take orders from others, including how to wear your hair on duty. (And glam girls, listen up: no make-up either.)

Amazing Disasters

Being a firefighter, you'll learn what a stupid lot the public and their animals can be! On top of hundreds of hoax calls from children who think they're funny, people call the fire service for reasons you won't believe! Have a laugh at this lot!

☛ People stuck in baths

☛ People locked out of their house

- Ponies stuck in rivers

- Cats stuck up chimneys (and other tiny gaps!)

- And yes, cats up trees. But no cat will ever come down if there's a bunch of strangers in yellow hats running around in its garden!

⊚ Tip from the Top ⊚

"Talk to other firefighters to find out about the job and prepare you for the interview. But don't expect any special treatment because you're a girl. The training is the same. You sleep in the same dorm at the station. And get fit!"

PAMELA OPARAOCHA, 32, FIREFIGHTER

Other Careers in the Fire Service

Hundreds of skilled people work behind the scenes to make sure a top notch fire service runs smoothly. People who are patient and good at calming others down in a panic situation are needed to answer emergency calls in the control rooms. There are loads of jobs in health and safety, recruitment and training, and administration. People working in press and public relations make sure the media and schools know about fire safety.

Other active jobs that involve helping others are in the army, navy and police force. Today, 70 percent of jobs in the army can be done by a woman, from vehicle mechanic and electrician to aircraft technician and gunfitter. Ask your careers advisor for more information.

Chapter 8
MOVIE STAR

★

Movie Star

So you want to be the toast of Hollywood, the talk of the town, the next big thing, the starlet the paparazzi adore, a glittering mega-star with Brad and Leo pestering you with text messages? Join the club, honey. Unfortunately, you share your dream with millions of girls. Every year, wannabe actresses pour into LA, home to the biggest movie studios in the world. They wait on tables on Sunset Strip, where the movers and shakers of the film industry make deals over Caesar Salad. And they work until they get a break, which takes a mix of talent, determination and a lotta luck. I'm just warning you about the competition. It's kinda high (that's what they call an understatement!), but if you want to act, go for it girl! You've got as good a chance as the next person. Just do it because you love it, not because you expect to be famous. But you never know!

Glam Factor	5
Brain Factor	2
Travel Factor	5
Money Factor	5
Stability Factor	0

Have I Got the Right Personality for the Job?

> "As an actress, you've got to be very tough or the competition just eats you up. It's not like you arrive in LA, smile a lot and everybody loves you. You have to go through a lot of horrible rejection until you get the right role."
>
> SARAH MICHELLE GELLAR

You need a certain amount of arrogance to be an actress. You've got to be really confident and believe strongly in yourself. Self-discipline and total commitment are everything, as it's up to you to get out there and compete for work. Getting an audition or interview is hard. Getting the part is harder. You can't take rejection personally and you can't be a quitter. A thick skin will come in very handy, as will the ability to pick yourself up and persevere.

> "For all their outward confidence, actors are often insecure and crave acceptance at the same time. A good actor is observant and sensitive to the things around them."
>
> JO STOCKHOLM, ACTRESS

It's a sad fact that you won't always be judged by your talent and personality. There are still far fewer interesting parts for women than there are for men. Casting decisions are based on appearance, whether you're male or female. But with money men and male directors making the casting decisions, women are judged on their body image much more than men. Once a Hollywood actress hits 35, her career is in danger. Even talented and beautiful actresses such as Sharon Stone and Susan Sarandon have difficulty getting decent roles!

> "How can anyone be as thin as we can? We have trainers to work us out. We have specially prepared meals."
>
> SARAH MICHELLE GELLAR

Melissa Joan Hart was understandably furious when she was asked to lose weight for her role in Drive Me Crazy. "It's so wrong. I'm comfortable with myself and I think life's too short to worry about body image! I threw a fit!"

Getting Started

Many actresses start in theatre to get as much experience of acting in front of an audience as possible. Take part in school plays, join a local youth theater group or set up your own drama group. Find out about the local amateur dramatics society. Take the initiative and get together with a group of friends, read plays and ask your school to

MOVIE STAR

put them on. If you choose plays by women, such as Caryl Churchill or look for women's theater companies, you'll have better parts to play. Try and do something about it by writing and directing yourself! Another option is to go to one of the open auditions for one of the youth theaters.

It's important to get an education and have skills to fall back on because acting is the most unstable career you could choose. Many actors have long periods without work. Don't limit your options too early.

"I make sure I don't miss out on the important things. I always try to go on school trips and I've got my prom and graduation coming up. Ten years from now, I would like to have gone to college, become a director and produced a movie from a book that I really like."

KIRSTEN DUNST ON WHY SHE TAKES HER EDUCATION SERIOUSLY

If you want to work in film or TV, you'll need an agent and going to a good drama school is the best way to get a good agent. (Having an agent is less important in theater.) If an agent takes you on, it's their job to find you parts. In return, you have to give them a cut of your salary.

Going to drama school is a popular path into acting. RADA, Italia Conti and The London Academy Of Music and Dramatic Arts (LAMDA) in the UK and The American Academy of Dramatic Arts, in Pasadena, and La Guardia School of Performing Arts, in New York, are among the best in the world. Many of the top drama schools are based in London. However, ask your careers advisor about courses across the country and look in prospectuses. You can do a course at college to prepare you for drama school. Go to their end of year shows to see which schools you like. You will need to pass an audition and/or an interview to get in and you'll be competing with loads of other people. At the end of your training, you'll be required to put on a show, to which all the agents are invited. This is the best way to show agents what you can do.

> *Kate Winslet didn't go to drama school and Christina Ricci has never taken a single acting lesson. They are two of the most talented actresses out there today. But success stories like these are few and far between.*

If you want to start early, there are schools that accept children. Competition is fierce to get in and lessons are a mix of the regular curriculum and the performing arts. Many students have to live away from home, staying with families in the area, so they can go to these schools.

My Big Break

Sarah Michelle Gellar was eating ice cream with her friends in a New York City restaurant, when an agent gave her his business card. She was four! She went on to appear in hundreds of commercials before landing a part in TV soap in the States, All My Children, for which she won an Emmy Award. This gave Sarah and her mom the confidence to move to LA and really make a go of it. After lots of auditions, the right role came along as vampire slaying, Buffy. Now Sarah's CV is full of movie hits, including I Know What You Did Last Summer, Scream 2 and Cruel Intentions.

Drew Barrymore was six when she starred in ET, but her acting career started long before that! At the suggestion of a friend, Drew Barrymore's mom took her 11-month-old daughter to an audition for a TV commercial for Puppy Choice Dog Food. When the puppy bit her, Drew just laughed! She got the part.

Another early starter is Melissa Joan Hart. She got her first acting role at the age of four, in an ad for a bath toy called "Splashy."

Michelle Williams's role as Jen in Dawson's Creek helped her nab a part in Halloween: H20. Dawson's creator, Kevin Williamson was involved in the making of the movie. She may have job offers pouring in now but she started off making commercials for fabric softener.

Kirsten Dunst started making commercials at the age of three, but her big break came when she was just 11. She made her first movie, Interview with the Vampire, with Tom Cruise and Brad Pitt!

Do's and Don't's

Do: Get your education and another skill to fall back on.

Do: Get involved in local theater groups and see lots of theater productions and movies.

Do: Celebrate your own uniqueness. Every actress plays Lady Macbeth in a different way. Don't imitate others; be special.

Don't: Listen to anyone who says you've got your head in the clouds and you should get a "proper" job. If you're talented and committed, go for it! (Of course, you probably will need to get another job as well to support yourself.)

Don't: Take it to heart if you don't get a part. It just means you didn't fit the criteria for that particular role.

Hours

They're crazy. Actors can go for long periods without getting work. When it does come, they can be working 15 hours a day, for months on end. There's lots of waiting around in film and TV. You might be in a scene for half an hour, then have to wait seven hours in your trailer for the next one.

"I've got twelve more days after today and I've been working twelve days straight already. All I want to do is lie on a sunny beach some where in the Caribbean!"

MELISSA JOAN HART FOUND THE HOURS A TAD DIFFICULT WHILE FILMING DRIVE ME CRAZY

Salary

Show me the money! If you make it to the A-list, with the likes of Julia Roberts and Gywneth Paltrow, you will be raking it in. In case you thought TV won't bring in the mega-bucks, take note of what Jennifer Aniston gets paid. She earns a tidy $500,000 per episode!

Of course, many actors struggle for years. They take low paid evening jobs in bars and restaurants so they can audition in the daytime. But once you get your big break, the money's peachy.

Perks and Pitfalls

Perk: You're doing a job that's very creative and satisfying, which gives you the freedom to express yourself in a way you wouldn't normally do.

Perk: You can be seen as a role model and inspire others or just provide entertainment, escapism and enjoyment!

Perk: There are excellent opportunities to meet lots of interesting people and travel.

Perk: The money can be very nice, indeedy.

Perk: Fashion designers will be falling over themselves to dress you for the Oscars.

Perk: Love scenes with sexy men!

Perk: The glamour, the fame, the showbiz parties, mmwa mmwa, darling!

Pitfall: Getting parts isn't easy, the competition is stiff, and there's a lot of rejection.

Pitfall: There's no stability. You never know when your next job will come along.

Pitfall: You have to have the energy to work two jobs, probably for a long time: one to pay the bills and one to get your big break.

"I don't get jealous if I don't get a part. I really believe in fate and that if I lose a role, it wasn't meant to be. I had a ballet teacher say to me once, be 10 percent better than yourself, as opposed to anyone else, because then you're not spending your energy fretting about other people."

NEVE CAMPBELL

Pitfall: Filming schedules can be tough, long and totally not glamorous!

Pitfall: You have to be prepared to travel far from home for long periods and live out of a suitcase.

121

MOVIE STAR

Pitfall: You have to remember lines . . . damn!

Pitfall: There are few central parts for women. Be prepared for a lot of stereotyping.

Pitfall: If you become famous, say bye-bye to privacy and hello to harsh stories about you in the press.

Short Cuts to the Top

Be in the right place at the right time. If you're in a production, invite agents to come along! Get involved in drama as much as you can. You've got to be in a race to win it!

Being a model or pop star gives you a jammy head start. Cameron Diaz and Milla Jovovich were both models while pop stars, Whitney Houston and Madonna have both crossed over into acting.

Get a famous boyfriend, wear a dress that's barely there and flirt with the camera, baby! It certainly got Liz Hurley famous, or was it recognition for her superb acting talents? (Ahem.)

> ### ☉ Tip from the Top ☉
>
> *"Sometimes in this business, there's still that old fashioned attitude that women should be seen and not heard. I'm not one of those people. If I'm in your presence, you're going to hear me."*
>
> JADA PINKETT

Other Careers in the Movie Business

There are loads of creative and technical opportunities, working behind the scenes in the film industry. Make-up artist, costume designer, set designer, camera operator, scriptwriter, script editor, sound engineer, cinematographer, soundtrack composer, producer and director are just a few.

Why not become the next Jane Campion (The Piano, Holy Smoke) or Lynne Ramsay (Ratcatcher) and think about writing or directing? Sophia Coppola starred in Godfather Part III and never thought about becoming a director until she read The Virgin Suicides. It was Kathy Lette's book which inspired Sara Sugarman to direct Mad Cows. Speak to your careers advisor about screen writing and directing courses.

For a real insight into what goes on behind the scenes on a film set, why not become a runner? Runners do a bit of everything, from researching on the Web and picking up props to photocopying and making the tea and coffee. Basically, they run around making sure everyone's got what they need when they need it.

Look for good books about the movie and theater industries at your bookstore and library. Write to the contacts you'll find in these books. You'll probably have to follow up with phone calls. And start as a volunteer. The experience will be invaluable!

Chapter 9
CONSERVATIONIST
★

Conservationist

There was a time, not so long ago in fact, when people who cared about "green issues" were labeled hippies or crazy eco-warriors. If you said you wanted to make a career out of caring for the environment, you might have been told to get a proper job. Well, making the world a better place to live in is what I call a proper job. Conservation is a serious business and there are lots of ways to get involved. From marine biologist and forest park guide to pollution officer and campaigner for Friends of the Earth, the possibilities are massive. But nobody is in this one for the money. If money is your driving force, you might as well skip this chapter altogether. If, however, you want a meaningful, rewarding way to spend your life; one in which you may be able to change the world, then read on, sister!

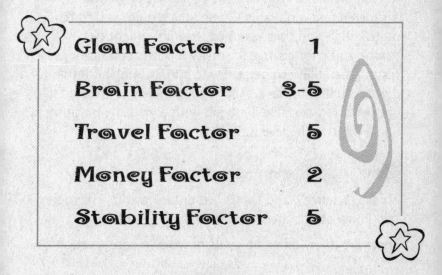

Glam Factor	1
Brain Factor	3-5
Travel Factor	5
Money Factor	2
Stability Factor	5

Have I Got the Right Personality for the Job?

If you're even thinking about the environment now, you obviously care. But if you want to make a career out of it, you've got to be passionate. If you're passionate about wildlife and nature, you could do a job that you really love. It takes a positive person to work in conservation. If you're not positive about the possibility of change, you'll be no use to anyone.

You should also enjoy working outdoors and traveling. People working in conservation can spend weeks in the office doing research, too, but there are plenty of interesting jobs that get you out and about. Many jobs involve talking with other people about why they should make a change to improve the environment, so being sensitive and assertive, hopefully even persuasive, helps.

It's important to work well in a team and that you are organized and motivated. Some jobs require you to be quite tough and thick-skinned, too. You might be campaigning for change for many months and never get a result. The ability to persevere in a frustrating situation is a good quality to have. Above all, people get involved in conservation because it's a job with a valuable purpose and a job they believe in.

Getting Started

Think, "science," and think, "voluntary work." The more you know about these two things the better.

There are many different levels of work in conservation. A

wildlife/park ranger, who is involved in conservation projects and the control of a forest's wild animals, such as deer and squirrels, needs skills above qualifications. The same applies to an Estate Worker, who does jobs such as hedging and tree felling. If you're interested in ocean life and becoming a marine biologist, you'll need a university degree and a further qualification, such as a MSc. or PhD.

Many people working at senior levels in conservation have degrees in Biology or Environmental Science. Geography is useful, too, as it includes the study of climate, geology and soils and how humans and their environments work together. If you want to become an environmental campaigner, other subjects to think about at higher level are Politics, Economics, Social Studies and Environmental Law.

Competition is high for jobs in conservation so many people get highly qualified to stand a better chance. There are always thousands of graduate environmentalists going for a small number of jobs. However, all you need to be concerned about right now is passing exams in science and mathematics.

Doing voluntary work is just as important as qualifications. It gives you experience and it shows you are committed. And anyway, if you love nature, it's really good fun!

> *"I got in touch with my local Wildlife Trust and worked for a summer as a volunteer. I absolutely loved it. I worked at a Marine Nature Reserve. It was a gorgeous bay with really shallow warm water. I'd show groups of children around the bay and we'd stick our heads in the water to look at the fish. It was brilliant!"*
>
> CLARE PERRY, WILDLIFE CAMPAIGNER AT THE ENVIRONMENTAL INVESTIGATIONS AGENCY (EIA)

The trick is to get involved. Get practical experience with your local Wildlife Trust or any other environmental organizations in your area. Why not get together with like-minded friends or set up your own group at school. Doing small things locally can make a big difference, such as clearing your local park or encouraging everyone in your street to recycle paper and glass. You could think about fun ways to raise money for a local environmental group or charity, stand up for your right to safe cycling lanes in the city, or write a leaflet for parents about the benefits of car sharing and walking to school.

On top of all that, handy skills to have for office-based jobs are computer literacy, a good telephone manner and research and writing skills.

"Living in cities, I realized that environmental issues are community issues. I wanted to tackle them at a grass roots level. There are a huge number of local issues that affect poor inner city families. They're the ones living in the areas that need regenerating. Everybody has a right to a clean environment, not just rich people."

MANDY GARNETT, GENERATION EARTH, THE BRISTOL ARM OF
FRIENDS OF THE EARTH

"I was always interested in wildlife and animals and I was good at science so that's what I studied. I wanted to be a vet or work for an animal protection agency, but studying biology made me aware of endangered species. I decided I wanted to help them more than domestic animals. And I knew I didn't want to work in a lab or spend more than 40 hours every week of my life doing something that wasn't worthwhile. I did a degree and lots of voluntary work to get here …it's not been easy."

CLARE PERRY, WILDLIFE CAMPAIGNER, EIA

"I always wanted to be a nurse but I did some voluntary work, taking inner city kids to the beach. They'd never seen a beach before and that made me think of doing something to raise awareness. Now I work for a charity, writing free environmental fact sheets for kids. It's our job to educate children so that they can do a better job than us."

JO LITTLEWOOD, PERSONAL ASSISTANT AT THE YOUNG PEOPLE'S TRUST FOR THE ENVIRONMENT AND NATURE CONSERVATION

Why Working in Conservation can be a Fairytale

Tiu Simila is a marine biologist living in Norway. After completing a degree in marine biology and a PhD studying Marine Mammals, she decided it was time to get out of the lab. She now lives on a boat so she can study killer whales!

"Little is known about killer whales. I've been following the whales for ten years and every year they bring me surprises. People make up fantastic stories about them, like they eat 13 dolphins a day! The fishermen thought the whales were eating all the herring, but I discovered that, when they go in for the kill, they actually leave most of the school behind. It's good to know that my studies have reduced the conflict between the fishermen and killer whales."

Why Working in Conservation can be a Nightmare

Mandy Garnett set up Generation Earth, a Bristol based arm of Friends of the Earth. Her job is to make the city a better place for everyone to live in, but sometimes her hands are tied.

"We were campaigning to stop the local council quarrying in the big park that everybody in the city uses. We took the council to court but the judge said that as members of the public, we had no say. Yet the park was given to the people of Bristol. We did a survey and found that 90 percent of the local people were against the quarrying of their only green haven. It took ages to go through the whole legal system. The frustrating thing was, another judge told us that the first judge had been totally wrong, by which time it was too late."

Hours

These really depend on the job. Some are 9-5, however, most people in conservation work really hard because they're passionate about what they do.

"I got a phone call in the middle of the night. I had to go and help stop this ship docking that was carrying genetically modified foods."

EMMA GIBSON, CAMPAIGNER FOR GREENPEACE

131   CONSERVATIONIST

> "We're campaigning against whaling in Japan and I had to research and write a report for the International Whaling Commission meeting. Sometimes I do work all hours. Something as important as that can't wait."
>
> CLARE PERRY, WILDLIFE CAMPAIGNER, EIA

Salary

Most jobs in conservation are low paid. Even if you're overloaded with qualifications and have a senior role, the money's not up to much, especially if you work for a charity.

> "If I was bothered about money, I wouldn't be able to do this job. No one does it for the money. But I've got the most amazing job; all my friends think that, too. I travel all over the world and meet all kinds of people."
>
> CLARE PERRY, WILDLIFE CAMPAIGNER, EIA

Perks and Pitfalls

Perk: You are doing something important and making a difference to the world.

Perk: You can be truly passionate about your job (how many people can say that?!).

Perk: The work can be unpredictable and exciting. Many people working in conservation talk about all their "amazing" and "unforgettable" experiences.

Perk: A lot of the work is outdoors and can involve travel overseas to exotic locations.

Pitfall: Other than manual jobs, jobs are few and the competition for them is high.

Pitfall: Jobs are often low paid.

Pitfall: Many conservationists hate, "the politics and paperwork." Often you'll be fighting authorities and governments to get things done and there's usually a lack of funds.

Pitfall: There's usually a lot of research involved, which can mean months of sitting in front of a computer, even stuffing envelopes all day.

Pitfall: You must be prepared to move around the country for a job, otherwise you're limiting your choices.

CONSERVATIONIST

✺ Tip from the Top ✺

"Don't think to yourself, 'No, it's other people who do that sort of thing. It only happens to other people.' Your worst enemy is yourself if you're not trying. You can have an unusual, exciting job!"

EMMA GIBSON, CAMPAIGNER FOR GREENPEACE.

Other Careers in Conservation

There are hundreds of jobs in conservation, all requiring totally different levels of skill. A Conservation Officer advises landowners and authorities on caring for their land and makes action plans for protecting natural habitats. They address problems such as coastal erosion and give talks to local groups or students. To do this job, you'll need a degree in a subject such as Biology or Geography and lots of experience as a volunteer. Have you thought about any of these? Pollution control officer, recycling officer, safety inspector, geologist, activist, geography teacher, science teacher, street cleaner, tree surgeon, landscape architect, Body Shop employee, river police, town planner, landscape architect, weather recorder/forecaster, forester, farmer, waste disposal technician, National Park warden, marine/freshwater biologist, microbiologist, pest controller, air quality controller, estate worker or florist. For info about all of these jobs, talk to your careers advisor!

Chapter 10
TV PRESENTER
★

TV Presenter

Do you imagine yourself as the freshest new face on TV? The host with the most, the presenter who interviews everybody who's anybody? If you've got the gift of the gab, a way with words, and a knock-out personality, you're in with a chance! If you think you can talk to anybody about anything, make the most boring topic sound totally interesting and hold the attention of millions of viewers with your natural girl charm, you were put on this earth to present! Go forth and conquer that black box! Just check your teeth for spinach first.

Glam Factor	5
Brain Factor	3
Travel Factor	4
Money Factor	4
Stability Factor	3

Have I Got the Right Personality for the Job?

You need a big personality for this one. If you're quiet and shy and you want to be a presenter, you'd better start coming out, now. Think confidence, think attitude and think different. It's unfair but true that you'll get an amazing headstart if you look like a model. But even if you do look like a model, if you can't hold an audience's attention, you're going nowhere fast. The golden rule is to be yourself. Viewers aren't stupid and they know a fake when they see one. Some presenters aren't particularly inspiring at all, but their naturalness endears them to the audience.

But there's more to it than naturalness and charisma. You do need good presenting skills and these depend on the type of presenting you're doing. As a rule, you must be articulate, able to present information in an interesting way, able to talk to and interview anybody and to never talk down to your audience. Having your own style is really important. Some presenters are terribly zany and wacky, some are dry and sarcastic, others are like the friendly girl next door. News presenters have to be serious and formal. Most presenters have to be able to switch from silliness to seriousness in a second. In live TV, being unpredictable really works and you'll need to think fast in case something goes wrong. You may also need to make up your own script on the dot if something goes wrong.

> *"A good presenter is themselves on screen. When you start out, you're 'presenting'; it's a front. You're a bit nervous and you're thinking about what you've got to say and where you've got to look. Then when you've done it a few times, your unique personality starts to show. I look back at old tapes of me now and cringe."*
>
> JEMMA JAMES, DISNEY CHANNEL

It's a competitive world in that box in front of the couch, so be a go-getter, be hungry, work hard and go for it!

Getting Started

There's no qualification to guarantee you a job like this and no right way of doing it. What's needed is dogged determination because there's a lot of competition out there. You can improve your chances by passing exams in subjects such as English, Drama and Media Studies. Some presenters have university degrees, and a post-grad degree in Broadcast Journalism; others have no qualifications at all. Some started off as secretaries, weather reporters, radio journalists, actresses, models or even sorting letters. Joining a local drama group will build your confidence and joining a youth film group will give you an idea of what goes on behind camera. There's no real training for this job because it's largely about your personality. It's not about acting or faking it.

You will see ads for presenting courses and workshops in the media jobs sections of newspapers and specialist newspapers for the broadcasting industry. These courses can be as short as one week and you leave with a showreel. However, they're not cheap and you can do it yourself.

A showreel is a tape of yourself presenting to the camera, so get your hands on a video camera. If none of your friends have one, ask your school; ask a tourist in the street! Three minutes of tape is long enough and don't worry if it's been filmed by your six year old sister – it's what you look and sound like that counts.

You'll need to show off your fab interview technique so find some interesting people to interview. If you live in the middle of nowhere and you can't find any, ask your friends! A good presenter has their own unique style. So just be natural, be yourself. Don't try and copy someone else's style. Don't imitate, innovate! Do lots of practicing first until you're happy with it. Think about the kind of presenting job you're going for. Children's TV presenters are lively and fun or a bit edgy. Sports presenters are knowledgeable about their subject and news presenters are more formal.

When your masterpiece is ready, start sending it to TV production companies. Some channels have in-house production, which means they make the programs, but many use programs made by production companies – watch out for the "endboard" at the end of a program to find who made it. Watch the end credits for the Executive Producer and the Production Co-Ordinator or Facilitator. These are the people who hire staff and have a lot of influence, so send your showreel to them. If you send it to Personnel, the right people may never see it. You can find the addresses in the phone directory or in specialist media guides like The Knowledge, and most will have a website with contact details. Most companies also have a work experience list, so ask if you can be put on it, and show them what you can do.

> "Some companies send your video back and say you're too young. (Some might not even return it, so be sure you make a copy to keep!) They might say you're not quite right or you're not what they're looking for but they'll keep you on file. I used to think they were lying when they said that but it's often genuine. Be persistent. Don't give up."
>
> JAMES McCourt, DISNEY CHANNEL

TV PRESENTER

While you're waiting for a response to your super-cool showreel, the most useful thing you can do is get work experience at a local radio station or television production company. Seeing for yourself what goes on behind the scenes will help you enormously. Another way 'in' is to get a job as a runner or a junior researcher. Jobs are advertised on company websites, in the media jobs sections of newspapers and in specialist newspapers for the broadcasting industry. Even if there isn't a position advertised, send your CV and a letter to TV production companies telling them why you'd make a red hot runner or researcher. They will keep you on file and if your application stands out, you may get an offer sooner than you think! Runners make sure everybody has what they need, that people are on time, and that their coffee cups are full. It's a good way to see how presenters relate to the director and the rest of the production team. Wear your Nikes because it involves a lot of running around!

Junior researchers gather background information for topics in the program. They spend a lot of time on the phone, on the Web, reading material and finding relevant people or locations of TV companies. Once you've got your foot in the door, you'll have a chance to prove yourself and let people know you're interested in presenting.

Did You Know?

Zoe Ball started off as a runner at the BBC and a researcher on The Big Breakfast.

My Big Break

"I made my own video in my back garden and sent it to everybody. At the same time, I was working in TV as a runner, then a researcher and then a production assistant. Presenting was my own little dream and I just kept on sending tapes and writing to people. It took years and hundreds of rejections before my break came, but one day Disney called up and asked me to audition!"

JEMMA JAMES, DISNEY CHANNEL

Do's and Don't's

Do: Have an alternative to fall back on. Presenting is one of the most competitive careers you can choose. And with models, sports people, and even Posh Spice giving it a try, it's even tougher!

Do: Get inside the industry by doing work experience or becoming a runner or researcher.

Do: Be natural on your showreel by thinking of the camera as another person.

Do: Talk to people doing the job in companies you'd like to work for. You can write to them and ask for advice.

Do: Be nice on your way up because you don't know who you'll meet on the way down!

Do: Be careful what you do to promote yourself. Stripping off for a men's mag doesn't work for everyone. Do you want to be viewed as a good presenter or a sex object first?

Do: Be confident and ambitious, but never arrogant.

Do: Be the best there is at your particular style of presenting. Even better, have your own unique style!

Do: Be yourself!

Don't: Give up on your dream but don't give up everything to follow that one goal.

Don't: Ever think there's something wrong with your personality if you don't get an audition. You'll be right for someone!

Don't: Think you have to be somebody else or speak a certain way.

"I used to think that no one would like my accent. But being yourself is a plus. So many presenters are the same, it's good to be different."

JEMMA JAMES, DISNEY CHANNEL

Don't: Fake it. Audiences can see through it, so be honest with the camera. This is not an acting job.

Don't: Try and cover up your mistakes if you're on live TV. It's better just to laugh them off. You don't have to be slick and perfect.

Don't: Go into presenting for the sake of it, because it's trendy or because you want to be rich and famous. It's hard work so you've got to really love it. If you love what you do, that will come across on screen, too.

Did You Know?

Denise Van Outen trained at The Sylvia Young Theatre School in London. Her classmates included Baby Spice and Nic and Nat All Saint.

Hours

Hours depend on the type of presenting you're doing, the time of year, the longevity of the show and so on. You could be working seven days a week for three months or just one day a week for three years! Summer and Christmas are busy for presenters in kids' TV and the Olympics and the World Cup will keep sports presenters working around the clock! A presenter who's just starting out might be given a contract to work for a three month period. If they really work hard and prove themselves, their contracts are extended.

Salary

Like any job, you start at the bottom but there is big potential for raking it in. A young presenter's first job could earn anything between £15,000 ($22,500) and £40,000 ($60,000), depending on the channel, the profile of the show and the hours of work. Once you build a reputation and get good ratings, you can demand more. Oprah and Roseanne have contracts worth millions!

Did You Know?

She may pose for the covers of predictable men's magazines but Cat Deeley is no muppet. This funny girl plays an active role in the writing and research of her shows and interviews.

Perks and Pitfalls

Perk: You can be yourself, entertain others and have a lot of fun!

Perk: The opportunities to travel and interview lots of interesting people are beyond incredible!

Perk: If you're successful, you can earn loads of money!

Perk: You're on TV!

Pitfall: There's a lot of waiting around before filming starts, whether it's waiting for equipment, sound and lighting to be right or waiting for a celeb to get over a hissy fit!

Pitfall: Hours can be long and working conditions not entirely desirable. You might be interviewing rock stars at a music festival but if it's outdoors, you'll be soaked, let's face it.

Pitfall: It's a fickle business. One minute you could be flavor of the month, the next minute, you're a nobody!

Pitfall: The double standards! As a woman, you'll be judged on the way you look much more than men. There's much more pressure on us to be glamorous. So break free from the stereotypes and show just how dull all those same, safe, blonde MTV babes really are! Don't be another boy pleaser, be a great presenter!

Short Cuts to the Top

* Become a model first. Caprice, Melanie Sykes and Live & Kicking's Emma Ledden all decided modeling was a bit boring and crossed over into presenting.

* Be a friend to the stars, then you can ask them all on your show. Posh Spice did it and even interviewed her own hubby!

* Get on TV as much as possible and show off as much as possible. From talent shows, talk shows and quiz shows to Blind Date or Singled Out – use any opportunity to do your party trick. You never know who's watching!

⊚ Tip from the Top ⊚

"The kind of person you are and your attitude count for more than what you've got on paper."

KATE SANDERSON, NEWSROUND PRESENTER

Other Careers in TV

There's plenty of fun going down on the other side of the camera. A whole team of creative bods make TV happen, from researchers, scriptwriters, camera operators, light and sound people, make-up artists, stylists, set designers, editors, producers, and directors! TV is one of the fastest growing industries today and women can do any job it has to offer. Many producers started off as runners or researchers at small, independent production companies and trained on the job. However there are Production Training courses available. Look out for these in specialist media newspapers.

TV PRESENTER

Personality Quiz

Remember, there are thousands of careers for you to consider. Finding the right one isn't all about skills and qualifications. It's about who you are. Think about what interests you, not what is expected of you. Think about what you like and what you don't like. You've probably got more hidden talents and strengths than you realize! Communication skills earned in a Saturday job, responsibility earned in a babysitting job, starting a football team outside school and being a good listener are all great assets! This isn't a quiz to tell you what job is right for you – but it should get you thinking about the kind of person you are.

Are you a people person?

1. You have just joined a new keep fit class. Do you:

A Stand at the back and avoid everyone's gaze.

B Join the big group at the front and start chatting.

C Walk up to the front of the class and introduce yourself.

2. You've been invited to a party but your best pal is on vacation and can't go. Do you:

A Stay at home. There's no way you're going out without her!

B Call the girl down the street, who you've been meaning to make friends with, and ask her if she wants to go with you.

C Hit the party without another thought – it'll be fun meeting new people!

3. Your English teacher wants some volunteers to stage a school revue. Do you:

A Keep your head down. Anything to do with drama is a no-no for you.

B Agree to help out behind the scenes.

C Offer to be the stage manager or the dazzling host!

How did you score?

A = 5   B = 10   C = 15

Low score = 15 – 20, medium score = 25 – 35, high score = more than 35

If you're a low scorer in this category, you need to work on those people skills! However, if you really like working alone, you could be self-employed as an interior designer, an illustrator, a writer, an organic farmer – many things! But you'll still have to talk to people!

Chapter to read: Famous Author.

If you got a medium score, you're clearly a people person with good communication skills. You might be suited to a career in teaching, in the police or in Public Relations (PR) which involves lots of meeting people, talking on the phone and making the most of your charm and persuasive powers. There are loads of jobs that need friendly, confident people who can talk to anybody!

Chapters to read: Magazine Editor, Conservationist, Firefighter and Vet.

If you're a high scorer, you are obviously an outgoing, sociable soul. Many jobs in the music business, television and advertising require confident go-getters like you. Other jobs you might think about are: children's entertainer, salesperson, sports agent or even a politician!

Chapters to read: Movie Star, Pop Star, TV Presenter and Supermodel.

Are you a leader or a team player?

1. You're going on a school trip to a museum and have been told to get into groups of six for the projects you'll have to complete while you're there.

Do you:

A Stick with your friends no matter what – you're not being left with the geeks!

B Suggest to your three friends that you make up a group with three others who have different skills and strengths.

C Organize the whole class into groups of six!

2. You've been asked to babysit your six cousins. Do you:

A Blankly refuse.

B Agree begrudgingly and send them to bed immediately so you can watch your favorite video.

C Turn up early with a list of fun stuff to do and a whistle!

3. You are working in a juice bar on Saturdays and the manager is off sick. Do you:

A Wait for one of the others to tell you what to do.

B Make a list of the jobs to be done and share them out fairly between you.

C Make the list and ask the other two to do them while you think up new strategies to improve business.

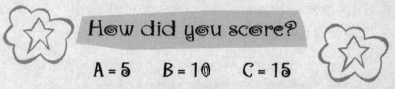

How did you score?

A = 5   B = 10   C = 15

Low score = 15 – 20, medium score = 25 – 35, high score = more than 35

Is your score low? Then you probably like to blend in the crowd. Well, come out girl because the ability to work in a team and share ideas is one of the best skills you can have!

Chapter to read: Famous Author.

A medium score means you're probably happy working in a team and sharing responsibility. Being able to get on and work with people is a vital quality in any job. After all, you could be working with lots of different personalities. Nurses, press officers, firefighters, shops assistants, environmental campaigners, sailors, army officers and people working in animal centers all need good team skills.

Chapters to read: Firefighter, Vet, Conservationist, Magazine Editor.

If you are a high scorer, you are clearly a natural leader and not afraid to take the initiative. You are willing to make that extra bit of effort to improve a situation. There are lots of important jobs out there for people like you. Have you ever thought of becoming a teacher, a manager of a large retail store, a manager of a sports team, a newspaper or magazine editor or a director? How about running a restaurant, a hotel or a youth center? A good leader works well in a team, entrusts tasks to and encourages others and carries responsibility well.

Chapters to read: Magazine Editor, Vet, Conservationist, Firefighter, TV Presenter.

How do you feel about change?

1. You're the new girl at school and it's do or die. Do you:

A Sulk in the corner and think about the friends you left behind.

B Get through the day by making a few friends.

C Embrace the idea of a new challenge!

2. You and your friends are planning a vacation. What's your idea of fun?

A Camping out in your family's back garden.

B A fortnight in Spain with lots of people you've never met.

C A round-the-world ticket for three months.

3. Which of the following phrases best describes you:

A You're a homebody. If you're at a sleep over, you'll call your mom to say, 'Hi'.

B You want to try new things but thinking about it can be a bit scary.

C You're hungry for adventure. You're not afraid to try anything!

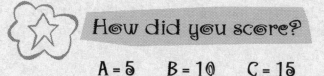

How did you score?

A = 5   B = 10   C = 15

Low score = 15 – 20, medium score = 25 – 35, high score = more than 35

If you scored low in this category, you might be a bit unsure about moving away from home to study or work. Think about going to college or getting a job in the area. There's no hurry to flee the nest yet!

If your score fell in the medium bracket, you have a healthy attitude to change and a *high score* in this section indicates that you're happy to try new things and treat them as a challenge. You might be suited to a job that involves lots of travel and meeting new people everyday. Models, entertainers, airplane cabin crew, travel reps and guides need these qualities. So do tour managers, journalists and teachers working abroad. People working in the media often have to move away to the big cities where many of the jobs are concentrated.

Chapters to read: Supermodel, Magazine Editor, Pop Star, Movie Star, Sports Champ and Conservationist.

How caring are you?

1. Your friend has split up with her boyfriend. Do you:

A Avoid calling her because she'll only be miserable.

B Call her, but swiftly move the conversation onto something more fun and interesting.

C Zip round there and take her out for pizza.

2. A kid is getting hassled by some bullies that you could see off, no sweat. Do you:

A Ignore it.

B Walk away and feel a bit guilty.

C Rescue the poor kid and take her for an ice cream.

3. A wild fox starts visiting your garden. It clearly needs medical care. Do you:

A Tell all your friends about it at school.

B Leave it some food and water.

C Call the animal rescue to come and give it the treatment she needs.

How did you score?

A = 5   B = 10   C = 15

Low score = 15 – 20, medium score = 25 – 35, high score = more than 35

Only if your score was high in this category do you care about others enough to take action. You might be suited to a career as a vet, a nurse, a doctor, an ambulance driver, a counselor, a teacher, a lawyer, or a kennel manager. Caring for others is a hugely rewarding career. It is not motivated by money, fame or status but a genuine desire or need to give. Doing voluntary work is a good way to help you decide what field interests you.

Chapters to read: Vet and Conservationist.

What motivates you?

1. There's a music festival near where you live. Which of the following are you most likely to do:

A Sell all your old junk in one of the stalls.

B Go along and have a great day out.

C Make a decorative backdrop for one of the performances.

2. Which of these pastimes would you find the most fulfilling:

A Shopping for designer gear.

B A bike ride on a sunny day.

C Painting a mural on your bedroom wall.

3. What's your idea of a perfect date?

A A meal at an expensive restaurant.

B Bowling.

C A picnic in a sunny meadow.

How did you score?

A = 5   B = 10   C = 15

Low score = 15 – 20, medium score = 25 – 35, high score = more than 35

If you're a low scorer, you might be quite money motivated or interested in a job that's high on glamour. You might be good at setting up your own business, working in retail or in fashion.

Chapters to read: Supermodel, Movie Star and Pop Star.

If you are a medium scorer, you're probably more active and fun loving. A career with a lot of time spent outdoors might suit you, such as countryside management or sports coaching.

Chapters to read: Sports Champ, Conservationist, Firefighter and Vet.

If your score was high, you are more motivated by creative fulfillment. A career in interior design, textile design, architecture or becoming a chef might suit you!

Chapters to read: Magazine Editor, Famous Author, Pop Star and Movie Star.

WANT TO KNOW MORE?

General

If you're not sure what it is you want to do, try these general career websites:

www.careerzone-uk.com

www.careersolutions.co.uk

and the Which? Guide to Choosing a Career, in good bookshops.

Try the personality test at
www.2h.com/Tests/personality.phtml

Think about what interests you and find out what jobs you'd be suited to in a computer program called PROBE. If your school careers library doesn't have one, call the Cambridge Occupational Analysts on 01362 688722 to find out where you can use it.

There's a great college personality quiz at
www.usnews.com/usnews/edu/college/cpq/coquiz.htm
which gives you good colleges to suit your needs. The questions will really get you thinking about what you're looking for. Or see the book the quiz was adapted from, called College Match: A Blueprint for Choosing the Best School for You! By Stephen R Antonoff, Ph.D and Marie A Friedemann, Ph.D (Octameron Associates, 1999)

Pop Star

Working In Music (1996, COIC)

All You Need To Know About the Music Business by Donald Passman

Vet

Contact The Royal College of Veterinary Surgeons at Belgravia House, 62-64 Horseferry Road, London, SW1P 2AP. Tel: 020 7222 2001, email: admin@rcvs.org.uk website at http://www.rcvs.org.uk

They have a useful leaflet that tells you about the job and where you can study.

For more info on Veterinary Nursing, contact the British Veterinary Nursing Association Ltd. Level 15, Terminus House, Terminus Street, Harlow, Essex CM20 1XA. Tel: 01279 450567 Email: bvna@compuserve.com

Good books: Careers Working with Animals (1997, Kogan Page)

Careers with Animals by Alan Shepherd

Working Outdoors by Alan Shepherd

Magazine Editor

You'll find a list of publishing companies and consumer magazines in the Hollis UK Press and PR annual, or the US version, The Literary Market Place. Names and telephone numbers of editors are listed. Your library should have a copy. You can send a letter requesting work experience to the recruitment officer or write direct to the editor of a particular magazine. The Writer's Market is a bit of a bible in the US. Inside you'll find the names of all the magazines and their editors, as well as info on the kind of articles they want.

Sports Champ

For info on everything from clubs, training and courses,

Contact The English Sports Council at www.english.sports.gov.uk or Tel.0207 273 1500. They have a handy, free publication, entitled Training and Educational Courses in Sport and Recreation. They also produce a book, Careers In Sport Compendium.

SPRITO at www.sprito.org.uk Tel: 0207 388 7755

Contact SPIRITO for their free guide, Sport and Recreation: How to Get In – A Guide For Students.

The Women's Sports Foundation at www.wsf.org.uk Tel: 0208 697 5370.

And find out how the celebs get fit at www.nrgize.co.uk

Good book: Careers in Sport by L Fyfe (1998, Kogan Page)

Supermodel

Career In Fashion by N Chapman (1998, Kogan Page)

Firefighter

Contact your local Fire Services Unit for more information.

Movie Star

You can help yourself by buying casting sheets and theatrical newspapers, such as The Stage (or Dramalogue, the actors' magazine in the US). The Stage has news of auditions for everything from musicals to film extras.

Spotlight is the UK directory, which lists actors. Contacts is the directory which lists everyone else, from casting agents to film and TV producers. Use Contacts to find out who an agent has on their books. If you like that actor's work, send that agent your details and a head shot and invite that agent to come and see you at your end of year show at drama school.

Both directories are available from Spotlight, 7 Leicester Place, London WC2.

Good books are The Film Actors' Complete Career Guide by Laurence Parke

Careers in the Theatre by J Richardson (1998, Kogan Page)

A Career In Broadcast, Film and Video (1996, Skillset – The National Training Organisation for Broadcast, Film and Video)

Light, Camera, Action: Careers in Film, Television and Video by Josephine Langhan

Great Careers for People Interested in Film, Video and Photography by David Rising

Wannabe movie directors should go to www.moviepitch.com for more info on how to make your idea a reality.

The Screen Writers' Work Book by Sid Field.

How To Make Money Script Writing by Julian Friedmann.

And reading actor's autobiographies will give you an interesting insight into show business. Good luck!

Conservationist

To find out about voluntary work, call your local Wildlife Trust. They can tell you about activities in your area and always need help taking care of nature reserves and monitoring wildlife. Ask your local library for their address or tel: 01522 544400.

Other useful places to try are: The British Trust For Conservation Volunteers, tel: 01491 839 766, the Environment Agency, tel: 0645 333 111 or visit www.environmentagency.gov.uk

For an idea of the opportunities in exotic locations, visit the Ecovolunteer website at www.ecovolunteer.org

If you want to start thinking about courses, ask your library for The Directory of Environmental Courses, published by the Environment Council. (www.theenvironment-council.org.uk)

Good books are Green Volunteers: the World Guide to Voluntary Work in Nature Conservation, published by Fabio Ausenda.

Working for the Environment by Barbara Buffton (1999, How To Books Ltd)

Careers in Environmental Conservation by Robert Lamb

Working with the Environment by Tim Ryder

Working Outdoors by Alan Shepherd

Or visit www.eto.co.uk

For lots of cool and free information on all things green, contact the Young Peoples' Trust for the Environment. Tel: 01483 539600 or visit their website at www.btinternet.com/yptenc. They've got fact sheets on everything from endangered species to pollution.

TV Presenter

Careers in Television and Radio by M Selby (1997, Kogan Page)

And check out www.bbc.co.uk/jobs for more info about working in TV.